Spiritual Warfare as an Effective Missionary Method

edition afem
mission academics 38

William Mark Wagner

VTR

edition afem
herausgegeben vom
Evangelischen Arbeitskreis für Mission, Kultur und Religion
von
Prof. Dr. Thomas Schirrmacher, Prof. Dr. Bernd Brandl
Friedemann Knödler und Thomas Mayer

Die **edition afem** besteht aus fünf Reihen: **Mission classics** wollen klassische Texte der Mission wieder neu zugänglich machen; **mission academics** bietet Forschungsarbeiten zur Missiologie; in **mission scripts** werden Textsammlungen, Arbeitsmaterialien und kleinere Arbeiten aufgenommen, und in **mission reports** werden Tagungsberichte veröffentlicht. Daneben gibt es noch die Reihe **mission specials**, in der Sonderveröffentlichungen aufgenommen werden.

Bibliographische Information der Deutschen Nationalbibliothek
Die Deutsche Nationalbibliothek verzeichnet diese Publikation in der Deutschen Nationalbibliographie; detaillierte bibliographische Daten sind im Internet über http://dnb.d-nb.de abrufbar.

ISBN 978-3-95776-064-7
ISSN 0944-1077

© 2017
VTR (Verlag für Theologie und Religionswissenschaft),
Gogolstr. 33, 90475 Nürnberg, http://www.vtr-online.com

Umschlaggestaltung: VTR
Satz: Friedemann Knödler

*To
my wife
Carrie
and my daughters
Kate and Natalie*

Contents

Preface 9

Chapter I:
Introduction to and Explanation of the Study 11
    Hypothesis of the Study 15
    Purpose of the Study 15
    Objectives of the Study 15
    Methodology of the Study 16
    Preliminary Considerations 16
    The Plan of the Study 18

Chapter II:
Cultural Themes 19
    Introduction 19
    Cultural Themes in the Study of Anthropology 19
    The Cultural-Theme Model 22
        A Definition of Culture 22
        A Definition of Worldview 24
        An Analysis of the Cultural Themes 24
        Summary 36
    The Impact of Cultural Themes on Individuals and Their Society 37
        The Nature of "People Groups" 37
        The Nature of the Cultural Theme's Influence 40
        Summary 47
    The Impact of Sin on Cultural Themes 48
        The Basic Disposition of Culture Themes 48
        The Extent of Sin's Influence on Cultural Themes 50
        The Nature of Sin's Influence on Cultural Themes 53
        Conclusion 57
    The Impact of Cultural Themes on a People Group's Receptivity to the Gospel 57
        Cultural Themes as Vehicles of Assistance 57
        Cultural Themes as Vehicles of Hindrance 58
        Missiological Responses to Hindering Themes 59
        Summary 60
    Conclusion 60

An Analysis of Existing Approaches for Dealing with the Demonic
Powers in Structures 132
   Walter Wink's 'Sociopolitical Action' Model 132
   Johann Howard Yoder's 'Contrast Society' Model 133
   Michael Green's 'Interdependent' Model 134
   C. Peter Wagner's 'Third Wave' Model 135
   An Evaluation 135
The Transformational-Encounter Model 137
   Encounters and Transformation 137
   The Transformation Process 140
Conclusion 147

Chapter VI:
Conclusion 148

Bibliography 150

Preface

The idea for this study grew out of my personal experiences of living and working with resistant people groups in Europe. I found that in many cases that people were resistant not because they rejected the gospel message as such, but because their cultural conditioning interfered in fully grasping the message of the gospel. As I began studying cultural anthropology, I became aware of the extent to which a society's worldview assumptions shape a person's life and his or her perception of the gospel. As I began to explore the relationship between a person's worldview and his or her level of resistance, I came across Morris Opler's cultural theme concept, which provided me an anthropological framework of understanding the relationship. At the same time, I began reading the works of Charles Kraft, C. Peter Wagner, and Paul Hiebert, which introduced me to the various aspects of strategic-level spiritual warfare and provided me a theological and missiological framework for understanding the demonic powers and their influence on individuals and their cultures. I began investigating the correlation between the cultural-theme concept and spiritual warfare. Through my studies and various cross-cultural ministry experiences, I found that cultural-theme strongholds are a reality and that by overcoming these theme strongholds a person's receptivity to the gospel increases. My hope is that the dissertation will provide insights and helps for missionaries and mission agencies to break through people's resistance so that the effectiveness of frontier missions can be increased.

Matters of style in this dissertation conform to the fifth edition of Kate L. Turabian, *A Manual for Writers of Term Papers, Theses, and Dissertations*. The dissertation was produced with the utilization of an IBM compatible computer, Hewlett Packard Laser printer, and Word Perfect 5.1 software.

Scripture quotations are taken from *The Holy Bible: New American Standard Version*, copyright 1960, 1962, 1968, 1971, 1973, 1975, 1977 by The Lockman Foundation.

The study would not have been possible without the inspiration, encouragement, and help of a number of people. I want to begin by thanking my professors at Southwestern Baptist Theological Seminary for providing the education and spiritual formation, which have inspired me and helped me in writing this dissertation. I especially want to thank Dr. Ebbie Smith for his encouragement, guidance, and practical help as my dissertation supervisor. I am indebted to Dr. Smith for his special effort in helping me complete the project. I also want to thank Dr. Daniel Sanchez for his seminars, which encouraged me to pursue this topic.

Throughout my studies there have been many people who have stood behind me and have supported my project. I would like to mention a few whom without their support the project would not have been possible. Foremost I want to express my gratitude to my parents Bill and Sally Wagner, who have supported and encouraged me in numerous ways throughout my studies. I am truly thankful to my wife's family for their continuous support. I especially want to mention Vivian Menees Nelson, who enabled me, through her generous assistance, to take the time out I needed to complete the dissertation. I also want to thank Robert E. Menees, Sharon Baker, Grant W. Merritt, and my grandmother Phyllis Crook for their support.

I want to express a special gratitude to the Waldersee Baptist Church and the Isernhagen Baptist Church who made many sacrifices on my behalf to provide me with the needed time for writing the dissertation. Thank you to all those members who stood behind me and believed in me. I want to thank Donna Smith for her help and patience in typing and putting the dissertation together.

Finally, I want to express my deep appreciation and love to my wife Carrie who always believed in me and supported me through good and bad times. It was because of her love, friendship, encouragement, and assistance I was able to complete this project.

Chapter I
Introduction to and Explanation of the Study

One of the most intriguing and important questions facing missiologists today revolves around the question of why some groups of people (people groups) demonstrate a greater receptivity to the gospel than do others. This question and efforts to understand and respond to factors of receptivity/resistance have engaged and continue to engage all who seriously seek to evangelize the peoples of the world.[1] Missiologists seek to understand the factors that lead to resistance and seek to eliminate or overcome these hindrances to the acceptance of the gospel. Equally important, missiologists seek to recognize receptivity and reap the spiritual harvest this openness provides.

The Apostle Paul expressed the Christian purpose as working with God to help free humans from the power of Satan and to guide them to God's forgiveness. He wrote: "… I am sending you, to open their eyes so they may turn from darkness to light and from the domination of Satan to God, in order that they may receive forgiveness of sin and an inheritance among those who have been sanctified by faith in Me" (Acts 26:17b-18 NASB).

Like Paul, each Christian and every Christian group remain mandated to the ministry of working with God to open the eyes of the spiritually blind and to help them break free from Satan's bondage and domination so that they may receive forgiveness of their sins and freedom in Christ. Believers are called to go to the nations, proclaim to them the full gospel of Jesus Christ, and guide them to discipleship with Jesus (Matt. 28:18-20).

Those who heed this call and seek to "open the eyes of the spiritually blind" soon realize that both individuals and groups differ in their receptivity or resistance to the gospel. Whereas some groups welcome the message with open arms, their opposition – even fierce opposition – to Christ and his way of life can characterize other groups. The question that continues to haunt missiologists is: What makes the difference between the receptive and resistant peoples? What causes some groups to resist the message? How can those involved in evangelism deal with the problems of resistant peoples? In other words, what leads to resistance in people groups and what can be done about it?

---

[1] An excellent overview of the receptivity and resistance and issue is found in Charles Van Engen, "Theological Reflection with Regard to the Resistant," paper presented at the Evangelical Missiological Society, San Francisco, 20 November 1997.

Increased resistance (or receptivity) can emerge from a number of different factors and the interaction of these factors. Understanding and dealing with resistance and receptivity occupies much missiological thinking and provides a theological impetus underlying the study of missiological anthropology. Contemporary missiological writings suggest at least three different factors that interrelate to produce, in groups, acceptance of or rejection of the gospel.

One factor, which must be seen as primary to a group's resistance relates to the fact of human sinfulness and the weakness of human "flesh". This inner drive and inclination leads humans to live separate from God, in rebellion against God, and even to active participation in evil. Human depravity, the tendency to sin, lies at the root of all forms of resistance to the message. Charles Van Engen points out that a missiological and theological understanding of resistance or resistant people must be grounded biblically in recognition of human sinfulness. This recognition must reflect the way humanity spiritually and relationally rejects God's loving self-disclosure to humankind.[2]

A second factor in developing receptivity and resistance relates to sociological, cultural, and communication factors. The emphasis on these social factors can be clearly seen in the Church Growth Movement's teaching of the important role such factors play in the missionary context. Donald A. McGavran declares that

> Since church growth takes place in the multitudinous societies of mankind, essential to understanding it is an understanding of their structure. Men exist not as discrete individuals, but as interconnected members of some society. Innovation and social change, operating in particular structures, play a significant part in determining the direction, speed, and size of the move to the Christian religion ... The influence of social structure on church growth is great. It can hardly be overestimated.[3]

Worldviews, traditions, values, customs, norms, power structures, language, and other factors in communication perpetuate and deepen a person's or group's resistance (or receptivity) to the gospel.

Recently, the Spiritual Warfare Movement has reemphasized a third factor in resistance, that is, the work of Satan and his legion of powers. These demonic powers constantly seek to blind people to the truth of the message of Christ. C. Peter Wagner, a leader in the Spiritual Warfare Movement, believes that the Devil directly and explicitly obstructs the evangelization of the lost and that

---

[2] Van Engen, 2.

[3] Donald A. McGavran, *Understanding Church Growth*, rev. ed. (Grand Rapids: William B. Eerdmans, 1980), 207, 222.

God has provided ways for Christians to remove many of these demonic related obstacles to evangelization through prayer and spiritual warfare.[4] The Lausanne Covenant of 1974 affirms that Satan and his forces constitute a major force in the struggle to evangelize people. The Covenant states, "We believe that we are engaged in constant spiritual warfare with the principalities and powers of evil (Eph. 6:12), who are seeking to overthrow the Church and frustrate its task of world evangelization (2 Cor. 4:3-4)."[5]

These three factors coincide with the three forces mentioned in the letter to the Ephesians (2:1-3) that keep unbelievers in bondage – that is, the flesh, the world, and Satan. Working together under the overall coordinating efforts of Satan and his powers, these forces lead to various types of strongholds and various levels of resistance among peoples.

An important part of sharing Christ with persons and groups of persons relates to dealing with the strongholds of resistance. Part of the mission mandate consists of overcoming (in the Spirit of God) these forces, barriers, and factors that keep people blinded to the Truth. This effort includes helping people deal with those issues and factors that make them resistant to the gospel and to guide them to move along the scale from resistant to receptive.

Resistance/Receptivity Scale[6]

-5 -4	-3 -2	-1 0 +1	+2 +3	+4 +5
Strongly Opposed	Somewhat Opposed	Indifferent	Somewhat Favorable	Strongly Favorable

In dealing with these factors that influence receptivity and resistance, some studies seem to center on one or the other of the previously mentioned factors. The Church Growth Movement has placed great emphasis on sociological factors while missiological anthropology has emphasized cultural barriers. The Spiritual Warfare Movement has considered strongly the spiritual and demonic barriers. Most studies on evangelism either center exclusively on or deal extensively with the sin barrier.

---

[4] C. Peter Wagner, *Confronting the Powers* (Ventura, CA: Regal Books, 1996), 25.

[5] "The Lausanne Covenant: Lausanne, 1974" in *New Directions in Mission and Evangelization 1: Basic Statements*, ed. James A. Scherer and Stephen B. Bevans (Maryknoll, NY: Orbis Books, 1992), 258.

[6] Edward R. Dayton and David A. Fraser, *Planning Strategies for World Evangelization* (Grand Rapids: Eerdmans Pub., 1980), 178.

A number of recent studies have sought to present some combination or relationship between the different factors and to combine these three factors in trying to understand and deal with a group's level of receptivity to the gospel.[7] Some studies have begun to focus specifically on the relationship between cultural structures and demonic influence as a factor in resistance.[8]

One further factor influencing receptivity has thus far been inadequately considered – that is, the relationship between worldview assumptions, also referred to as cultural themes, and the demonic powers. Studies have shown that worldview and its cultural themes play key roles in the receptivity or resistance of individuals and people groups.[9] Equally clear is the fact that demonic forces are active in hindering the gospel. How do these forces, the cultural themes and the satanic influences, work together to influence the receptivity of a people, and how can this situation, when it happens, be addressed and overcome? This exact question constitutes the driving and central issue of this study.

---

[7] Some of the more recent studies include: Clinton Arnold, *3 Crucial Questions about Spiritual Warfare* (Grand Rapids: Baker Books, 1997); *Powers of Darkness* (Downers Grove, IL: InterVarsity Press, 1992); John D. Robb, *Focus! The Power of People Group Thinking* (Monrovia, CA: MARC, 1994); A. Scott Moreau, *Essentials of Spiritual Warfare: Equipped to Win the Battle* (Wheaton, IL: Harlod Shaw Pub., 1997); Klaus W. Müller, ed. *Mission als Kampf mit den Mächten: Zum Missiologischen Konzept des "Power Encounter"* (Bonn, Germany: Verlag für Kultur und Wissenschaft, 1993); Timothy M. Warner, *Spiritual Warfare* (Wheaton, IL: Crossway Books, 1991); and C. Peter Wagner and Douglas Pennoyer, eds., *Wrestling with Dark Angels* (Ventura, CA: Regal Books, 1990).

[8] Some of these writers include: C. Peter Wagner, "The Visible and the Invisible," in *Breaking Strongholds in Your Cities*, ed. C. Peter Wagner (Ventura, CA: Regal Books, 1993), 50-79; F. Douglas Pennoyer, "In Dark Dungeons of Collective Captivity," in *Wrestling with Dark Angels*, ed. C. Peter Wagner and F. Douglas Pennoyer (Ventura, CA: Regal Books, 1990), 250-70; John Robb, "How Satan Works at the Cosmic Level," in *Behind Enemy Lines*, ed. Charles H. Kraft and Mark White (Grand Rapids: Vine Books, 1994), 165-98; Klaus W. Müller, "Power Encounter als Missions-Strategisches Konzept," in *Mission als Kampf mit den Mächten: Zum Missiologischen Konzept des "Power Encounter"*, ed. Klaus W. Müller (Bonn, Germany: Verlag für Kultur und Wissenschaft, 1993); Walter Wink's trilogy *Naming the Powers* (Philadelphia: Fortress Press, 1984); *Unmasking the Powers* (Philadelphia: Fortress Press, 1986); *Engaging the Powers* (Minneapolis: Fortress Press, 1992); and Paul G. Hiebert, "The Gospel in Our Culture: Methods of Social and Cultural Analysis," in *The Church between Gospel and Culture*, ed. George R. Hunsberger and Craig van Gelder (Grand Rapids: Eerdmans Pub., 1996), 139-57.

[9] See Charles Kraft, *Anthropology for Christian Witness* (Maryknoll, NY: Orbis Books, 1996); and Louis J. Luzbetak, *The Church and Cultures* (Maryknoll, NY: Orbis Books, 1988).

Chapter III:
The Relationship of Demonic Powers to Cultural Themes 62

Introduction 62
An Analysis of the Powers / Theme Relationship 63
    Definition of Terms 63
A Biblical Analysis of the Power / Theme Relationship 65
    An Evaluation of the Biblical Teaching on the Demonic Powers'
    Relationship to Structures and Cultural Themes 71
    An Analysis of Current Interpretations of the Powers/Theme Relationship .. 83
A Suggested Model for the Powers / Theme Relationship 94
    The Nature of the Powers / Theme Relationship 94
    The Purpose of the Demonic Powers 95
    The Nature of the Demonic Powers' Influence on Cultural Themes 96
    The Nature of Theme-Related Demonic Strongholds 98
Conclusion 102

Chapter IV:
Spiritual Diagnosis 103

Introduction 103
An Analysis of Spiritual Mapping 104
    A Definition for Spiritual Mapping 104
    Current Understandings of Spiritual Mapping 106
    An Evaluation of Spiritual Mapping 109
    The Spiritual Diagnosis Model 113
A Spiritual Diagnosis Model for Profiling Theme Strongholds 114
    Setting up the Research 114
The Research 117
    Pulling the Research Together 126
Conclusion 128

Chapter V:
Overcoming the Demonic Cultural-Theme Stronghold
through Transformational Encounters 129

Introduction 129
An Analysis of Existing Approaches for Transforming Cultural Themes 129
    Replacing Transformation 130
    Planting Transformation 130
    Retaining Transformation 130
    Restoring Transformation 131

Hypothesis of the Study

This study contends that cultural-theme strongholds present significant barriers leading to resistance to the gospel among given cultural groups. Further, the student contends that these cultural-theme strongholds emerge partially from distortions of the cultural themes. These distortions spring from the sinful nature of fallen humankind, from cultural entities, from the action of Satan and his demons, and from the direct action of demonic forces upon the dominant cultural themes of a people. The corruption of the basic themes in the group's worldview establishes strategically significant barriers, which lead to the people group's increasing resistance to the gospel.

Overcoming this stronghold of distorted cultural themes and returning the themes to their divinely intended content and expression can break the demonic grip the stronghold maintains and allow the people group as a whole to move significantly along the path to receptivity on the receptivity / resistance scale. Such a restructuring of the worldview and the themes within it will provide a natural path for both introducing and contextualizing the gospel for the particular cultural group. Identifying and guiding people to overcome the cultural-theme strongholds through God's power can exert significant impact and power in evangelistic strategy.

Purpose of the Study

The hypothesis of the study leads directly to its twofold purpose. First, it is to help cross-cultural workers and the peoples with whom they minister to identify the cultural-theme strongholds that exist in their cultures and the degree to which these themes might be distorted due to demonic powers. Second, the study seeks to help workers and people to break the bondage of the strongholds and satanic powers. Breaking the power of the strongholds and restoring the themes to their divinely intended natures and functions will allow and guide individuals and people groups to move away from resistance and toward receptivity. Further, this effort to identify and overcome distortions of cultural-theme strongholds will impact not only the basic receptivity of the group but also the methods by which the message is presented. The concept will impact mission strategy and method.

Objectives of the Study

Based on the hypothesis and the purpose of the study, the effort has a fivefold statement of objectives. First, the study analyzes the concept of cultural-theme strongholds and demonstrates how the reality of this concept affects a people's reception of the gospel. Second, the study investigates the role of demonic powers in distorting and maintaining these disturbed cultural themes. Third, the study establishes a methodology for diagnosing and identifying the cultural-theme strongholds. Fourth, the study seeks to establish a strategy for dealing with distorted cultural themes that relates both to the natural components and to the demonic dimensions. Finally, the study approaches the effects that cultural themes have on missions and demonstrates how overcoming these strongholds can increase the effectiveness of missionary activity.

Methodology of the Study

The methodology followed by this study integrates four distinct fields of investigation. It emerges from the field of missiology. The primary concern is that of discovering more effective ways to conduct missionary work. Secondly, the study relates to and relies heavily upon cultural anthropology because the basic concept of cultural themes is an anthropological concept. The relationship of anthropological theories to missions stems from the field of missionary anthropology.

The third field consulted by this study stems from theology. The goal seeks to contextualize the gospel to cultures and to relate theology to the gospel. The focus remains that of finding a model and understanding of resistance that is compatible with the theology of Scripture.

Finally, the study deals with power ministries – evangelism, church growth, perfecting efforts, and humanitarian concerns. This spiritual component of the study relates to a relatively new field of investigation – that of power evangelism and other factors in the contemporary *Spiritual Warfare Movement*. The study focuses on the issue of the spiritual dimension through prayer, power encounter, and signs and wonders. Within the context of the study, there is an underlying dialogue between the four fields. The study incorporates and combines the concerns, methodologies, and insights of the fields in order to create a more holistic model and strategy for missionary efforts.

This study is foremost theoretical. It analyzes and evaluates existing theories and teachings and uses these insights in developing the cultural-theme stronghold concept. The ultimate goal is the creation of an acceptable synthesis between anthropological theory, theological concepts, missiological goals, and missionary methodologies as well as power-ministry practices.

Preliminary Considerations

The presentation of the study follows definite parameters. While acknowledging that there exist numerous interrelated factors in the presence and degree of resistance of a group to the gospel, this study concentrates on one of these factors, the distortion of cultural themes by human sinfulness and by demonic powers. It will discuss the other factors of resistance only as they relate directly to the cultural theme concept. The study, while using insights from several fields, will use these insights only as they impact the topic at hand. Little effort will be exerted at proving the concepts from the other fields (anthropology, theology, power ministries). It is assumed that these concepts are founded within the disciplines in which they emerge. These concepts are analyzed and evaluated as they relate to the study of cultural themes.

Each topic is discussed as a part of the larger context of this study and not from the many interesting and vital directions that are possible. For example, the concept of cultural themes will be discussed as part of the fields of Configurationalism and Culture and Personality. The study will not deal extensively with other models of culture. In the same way, the discussion of demonic activity will be limited to strategic-level spiritual warfare concepts. The study seeks to show the relationship between cultural themes, sinful and demonic distortions of them, and the place of this concept for missionary activity.

The study's plan follows two basic assumptions. First, it is conducted solidly within the context of evangelical theology. The foundation for the entire effort accepts the premises set forth in the Lausanne Covenant of 1974. The divine inspiration of Scripture, as stated in this Covenant, forms a foundation for all that is thought and practiced in the study.

As a part of this biblical and evangelical foundation, the study assumes that Scripture provides proper and usable insights into the nature of demonic beings, their activities and intentions. There is no "demythologizing" of the biblical accounts of Satan and demons. Biblical teachings are paramount in the study.

Second, the study fully affirms the sovereignty of God. There is no intention in this study to create a man-made strategy for overcoming the barriers to the gospel. The study assumes that the proposed strategy will function in conjunction with the *missio dei*. The methods envisioned in this study must be understood as part of human response to the call for missionary activity. The underlying assumption is that God initiates and reveals the process, directs the research into the project, and implements the use of the model. Missionaries have the responsibility to plan the study, seek the methods, commit the entire effort to God, and await his timing and power for the action.

The study makes no claim to be a new and substitutionary method or approach to evangelism and contextualism. It seeks rather to present the method as complementary to the traditional models of evangelism and contextualization – to strengthen and enhance them. It is a complementary method, not a contrasting nor supplanting means.

The Plan of the Study

The presentation of the study divides into two major parts contained in five divisions or chapters. Chapter 1 introduces the topic and states the need for studying the cultural-theme stronghold as a resistance factor among people groups in missions. Chapters 2 and 3 comprise the first section, which analyzes the cultural-theme stronghold concept and shows how this concept relates to the resistance of peoples. This section of the presentation examines the cultural-theme concept, the nature of demonic powers and influences, and the interrelationships between the two.

The second major section, which includes chapters 4 and 5, establishes a strategy for dealing with the strongholds with the purpose of finding and maturing an environment of receptivity for the gospel. This goal will follow the plan of developing a research model which will guide in identifying and profiling the strongholds. This research section will be followed by a proposed strategy for breaking the bondage of the strongholds through transforming the cultural themes and overcoming the influences of the demonic powers. The focus of the study is that of finding means and ways to increase the effectiveness of cross-cultural evangelism.

The study has the goal of investigating one of the most significant and least discussed of the many factors involved in turning peoples to resist the gospel. It seeks to show that the cultural-theme stronghold reality significantly influences the perception and reception of the gospel. It further indicates that properly dealing with these distorted themes through God's power can improve the effectiveness of evangelism and contextualism.

Chapter II
Cultural Themes

Introduction

A society's perception, values, standards, attitudes, as well as its thinking and behavior patterns are shaped by its worldview, which is comprised of the society's deep-level assumptions, premises and basic beliefs, known as cultural themes.[10] The influence of the themes is far-reaching, deep-rooted, and all-inclusive. Missiologists are becoming more aware that cultural themes play a significant role in how a society and its people perceive and respond to the gospel. On one hand, they function as a helpful vehicle for introducing and establishing the gospel in a given society. On the other hand, they can become barriers to the evangelization and contextualization process, leading the society to resist and oppose the gospel. What are cultural themes? How do they function? How do they influence a society? And how do they impact missions?

This chapter will analyze the cultural-theme concept in light of its importance for missions. It will examine the nature, purpose, function, and expression of the themes and analyze the nature and means of the theme's influence. It will consider the impact sin has on cultural themes and show how sin creates a cultural-theme stronghold, which adversely affects the evangelism and contextualization processes. The purpose of this chapter is to show how cultural themes affect the individual, his or her society, as well as his or her response to the gospel.

Cultural Themes in the Study of Anthropology

Throughout the history of anthropological studies, various approaches for studying culture have evolved.[11] The evolutionary model, historicalism, and

---

[10] The cultural-theme concept, as developed by Morris E. Opler in his work "Themes as Dynamic Forces in Culture," *American Journal of Sociology* 51 (1945): 198-206, is an anthropological model which even though it has many critics, has proven useful for explaining and dealing with a culture's deep-level structures. This study will not deal with the issues surrounding its validity in anthropological studies. It will assume that this established model provides an adequate, fitting, and useful paradigm for explaining and dealing with the foundational structures of culture. The chapter will show how the deep-level structures of culture affect missions, based on the cultural theme model.

[11] This overview is based on Merwyn S. Garbarino, *Sociocultural Theory in Anthro-*

diffusionism all view cultures according to the nature of their development. The evolutionary approach perceives the differences in cultures based on their evolutionary development from the simple to the complex. Representatives include James G. Fraser, Leslie White, and Julian Steward. Historicalism, championed by Franz Boas, assumes that differences between cultures are a product of historical events and circumstances. Diffusionists such as Grafton Elliot Smith, William J. Perry, W. H. R. Rivers, Wilhelm Schmidt and those from the *Kulturkreis* school assume that cultures developed through the means of cultural borrowing and cultural diffusion.

The functionalist and structuralist approaches study culture and its components in terms of its function, its maintenance of the society as a whole, and the integrative relationship between the components. The functionalist approach grew out of the works of Emile Durkheim and was developed by Bronislaw Malinowski and Alfred Reginald Radcliffe-Brown. French Structuralism, led by Claude Levi-Strauss, searches for the innate structures in nature in order to determine the structures in society.

The 'Culture and Personality' approach uses psychological models and categories to understand culture. Representatives include Edward Sapier, Benjamin Whorf, Anthony F. C. Wallace, Francis Hsu, and Abram Kardiner. The most recent approach, cultural materialism, views the development of culture primarily in terms of the societies' material constraints (need for food, shelter, tools, machines, etc.). Marvin Harris is the primary proponent of this view.

Related to the 'Culture and Personality' approach is Configurationalism. It deals with society's cluster of traits and characteristics, and deep-level assumptions that identify it and set it apart from other cultures. Significant pioneers in this field include Ruth Benedict and Margaret Mead. Benedict sought to identify a single, dominant personality type that accounted for the uniqueness of that culture. Mead studied the relationship between personality and culture. She suggested that there were primary as well as secondary trends in a culture.[12]

---

pology: A Short History (Prospect Heights, IL: Waveland Press, 1977), 64-84; Luzbetak, 148-50; and Klaus Müller, "Geschichte der Ethnologie," in *Ethnologie, Einführung und Überblick*, ed. Hans Fischer (Berlin: Dietrich Reimer Verlag, 1992), 23-56.

[12] See Ruth Benedict, "Configurations of Culture in North America," *American Anthropologists* 34 (1932): 1-27; *Patterns of Culture* (Boston: Houghton Mifflin, 1934); Margaret Mead, *Coming of Age in Samoa* (New York: Morrow, 1928); and *Sex and Temperament in Three Primitive Societies* (New York: Morrow, 1935). Another significant pioneer in the field is A. L. Hallowell, *Culture and Experience* (Philadelphia: University of Pennsylvania Press, 1955).

During the 1940s and 1950s, a number of cultural character studies were conducted and various configuration models were developed. The most applicable and useful of these models is Morris Opler's cultural-theme model. He suggests that a culture is organized around a network of interrelated themes, which organize, stimulate, and control a society's thinking and behavior.[13] His cultural-theme concept will serve as the basis for the cultural-theme model presented later in this study.

Even though the number of anthropologically oriented character studies decreased after the 1950s, the interest in studying the core constructs of culture has continued through the present. Francis Hsu[14] and James Spradley[15] are among the more notable representatives that have adapted Opler's cultural-theme concept for their understanding of culture.

Configurationalism has its weaknesses and strengths. The main weakness is the study's tendency for oversimplification, which has often perpetuated unwarranted, superficial, and stereotypical characterizations of a society. The studies, furthermore, have a tendency to be idiosyncratic. The results of the character studies often differ from observer to observer.[16] Finally, an adequate study usually takes a great amount of time and research to arrive at acceptable and usable results. Even in light of these weaknesses, configurationalism has

---

[13] Morris E. Opler, "An Application of the Theory of Themes in Culture," *Journal of the Washington Academy of Science* 36 (1946): 137-65; Opler, "Themes as Dynamic Forces"; Morris E. Opler, "Component, Assemblage, and Themes in Cultural Integration and Differentiation," *American Anthropologist* 61 (1959): 955-64. For an overview of Opler's theme concept as it relates to missions, see Luzbetak, 276-91.

[14] In the tradition of Ruth Benedict, Hsu has focused on identifying a single dominant 'personality' trait in cultures. Francis L. K. Hsu, "American Core Values and National Character," in *Psychological Anthropology: Approaches to Culture and Personality* (Homewood, IL: Dorsy, 1961).

[15] James P. Spradley, *The Ethnographic Interview* (Fort Worth, TX: Harcourt Brace Javanovich College Pub., 1979; and James P. Spradley, *Participant Observation* (New York: Holt, Reinhart & Winston, 1979).

[16] The study of the Mexican town Tepoztlan by Robert Redfield became the center of much debate as Oscar Lewis restudied the same town, coming up with opposite conclusions from Redfield regarding the characteristics of the town's people. The reason for the difference was the orientation of the two researchers. Redfield studied the normative culture, whereas Lewis described the behavior of the people. Robert Redfield, *Tepoztlan: A Mexican Village* (Chicago: University of Chicago Press, 1930); Oscar Lewis, *Life in a Mexican Village* (Urbana, IL: University of Illinois Press, 1951). This comparison shows the impact which the approach and the researcher's preunderstanding have on the results of an ethnographic research. Garbarino, 71.

proven helpful in understanding the deep-rooted themes and structures of culture and has been useful in planning and carrying out culture change.[17]

The cultural-theme concept and other related configurational models have proven helpful in missions. Many missionary anthropologists, such as Louis Luzbetak, Paul Hiebert, Charles Kraft, and Daniel Shaw, are using the theme model to explain the deep-level structures of culture and to show how the gospel can be introduced into a culture.[18] An increasing number of missiologically oriented ethnographic studies are using the theme model as a basis for finding the most effective ways to contextualize the gospel in a given society.[19] Even though there are some valid concerns about the cultural-theme concept and other configurational models, these approaches have proven helpful for the task of evangelism and contextualization.

The Cultural-Theme Model

Cultural-themes are the basic assumptions and premises that make up a society's worldview, which in turn organize and shape all other aspects of the society's culture.[20] To understand better the cultural-theme model and its sweeping influence, this study will begin by looking at the concepts of culture and worldview.

A Definition of Culture

Each society has its unique culture and all human beings share in one or more cultures. There are a number of different definitions for culture.[21] Louis

---

[17] Garbarino, 73.

[18] Luzbetak, 249-91; Charles Kraft incorporates the theme concept in his discussion on worldviews in *Anthropology*, 51-68; also see P. Daniel Shaw, *Transculturation* (Pasadena, CA: William Carey Press, 1988); and Marguerite G. Kraft, *Worldview and the Communication of the Gospel* (Pasadena, CA: William Carey Press, 1978).

[19] Some of the ethnographic studies which have used the cultural-theme concept for missiological purposes include Daniel Shaw, *Kandila* (Ann Arbor, MI: University of Michigan, 1990); and William Conley, *Kalimantan Kenyah* (Nutley, NJ: Presbyterian & Reformed Pub., 1973).

[20] The study will differentiate between the concepts of culture and society. Culture refers to the structuring of life, whereas a society refers to the people who live within the structure. Charles Kraft, *Anthropology*, 40.

[21] See A. L. Kroeber and Clyde Kluckhohn, *Culture: A Critical Review of Concepts and Definitions*, vol. 47, no. 1, Papers of the Peabody Museum of American Archaeology and Ethnology (Cambridge: Harvard University, 1952). Most definitions of culture will presuppose a distinct approach or theoretical base and reflect a particular perspective or model. In this study, culture, worldview, and cultural themes

Luzbetak provides a definition that is well suited for missiological concerns, as well as for this study. Culture is "a plan consisting of a set of norms, standards, and associated notions and beliefs for coping with the various demands of life, shared by a social group, learned by the individual, and organized into a dynamic system of control."[22]

Luzbetak understands culture as an "ideational code", a mental construct consisting of a conglomerate of concepts and ideas. It is seen "as a shared communication network that sends messages along vast and elaborate interconnected routes. Culture is therefore an interwebbing of signs (bearers of messages and their meanings)."[23] It functions as a plan, strategy or blueprint which a society adapts for itself and which integrates, orders, and gives guidance to every aspect of a society's life. Economics, technology, social interaction, politics, religion, aesthetics, ethics, as well as behavioral and thinking patterns are shaped and structured according to this cultural plan.[24]

There are three levels of culture.[25] The individual building blocks of culture, which include the forms, shapes, signs, and symbols, without their prescribed meanings make up the surface level. It deals with the who, what, when, where, how, and what kind of culture. The second level assigns the function and meaning to the forms and symbols and provides a system of order on how each element in culture interrelates. The third level deals with the inner logic of a culture. It is a society's underlying values, norms, beliefs, assumptions, and themes which structure and organizes a society as well as serves as the starting point for its reasoning, thinking, reacting, and evaluative process. It is commonly referred to as worldview.[26]

---

will be defined to fit the missiological context.

[22] Luzbetak, 156.

[23] Ibid., 154. This understanding of culture is based on a symbolic or semiotic approach to anthropology, a subcategory of cognitive anthropology. Representatives of this approach to anthropology include Clifford Geertz, Mary Douglas, and Edmund Leach. Robert J. Schreiter has applied this approach to the contextualization process of the gospel in his book *Constructing Local Theologies* (Maryknoll, NY: Orbis Books, 1985).

[24] Kraft, *Christianity in Culture* (Maryknoll, NY: Orbis Books, 1979), 390-91.

[25] Luzbetak, 159, 223.

[26] Other terms used to describe the concept of worldview include 'concept of values', 'value orientation', 'core symbols', 'premises', 'ethos', 'genius', 'mentality of a society', 'inner logic', 'cognitive orientation', 'root metaphor', and the 'soul of a culture'.

A Definition of Worldview

The worldview is the 'central control box' of culture.[27] Charles Kraft defines worldview as

> the culturally structured assumptions, values, and commitment / allegiances underlying a people's perceptions of reality and their response to those perceptions ... It is included in culture as the structuring of the deepest level presuppositions on the basis of which people live their lives.[28]

A worldview organizes and shapes all aspects of the people's culture, orders their experiences, and gives meaning to their lives. It is the conglomeration of a society's basic and implicit assumptions, premises, and assertions which deals with the society's perception of reality, sets forth its understanding of morality, and establishes its basic values, commitments, ideals, and interests. It unites and organizes the various aspects of culture into an integrated system and gives the culture its unique configuration.[29]

Some of the premises and assumptions function as major dominant themes which guide and shape all the other areas of a culture and function as a primary driving force for the thinking process and behavior of a society. These cultural themes lie at the heart of culture and serve as the basic cornerstones for a society's worldview and its culture.

An Analysis of the Cultural Themes

A Definition of Cultural Themes

The term cultural theme was coined by Morris Opler to describe the distinct affirmations made by a society, which provide culture with its character, shape, and distinction. He defines cultural theme as "a postulate or position, declared or implied, and usually controlling behavior or stimulating activity, which is tacitly approved or openly promoted in a society."[30]

---

[27] For an in-depth look at the concept of worldview, see Michael Kearny, *World View* (Novato, CA: Chandler and Sharp, 1984); James P. Spradley and David McCurdy, "Worldview and Values," chap. 14 in *Anthropology: The Cultural Perspective* (New York: Wiley, 1975). For further discussion on worldview from a missiological perspective, see Luzbetak, 249-91; Kraft, *Anthropology*, 51-67 and 433-46; and Paul G. Hiebert *Anthropological Insights for Missionaries* (Grand Rapids: Baker Books, 1985), 45-50.

[28] Kraft, *Anthropology*, 52.

[29] Paul G. Hiebert, *Cultural Anthropology* (Grand Rapids: Baker Books, 1983), 369.

[30] Opler, "Themes," 198.

Luzbetak builds on this definition and defines cultural theme as "a basic set of generally consistent postulates and core attitudes and motivating forces that run more or less through the whole culture and that give the culture its character and dominant emotional tone."[31]

Spradley focuses on the integrative function of the cultural theme in his definition. He defines cultural theme as "any cognitive principle, tacit or explicit, recurrent in a number of domains and serving as a relationship among subsystems of cultural meaning."[32]

Based on the three previous definitions, this study will define cultural theme as a society's core cognitive principle, postulate, and assumption, which lies at the heart of the culture and integrates and organizes all other aspects of a culture into a coherent worldview. It is most commonly expressed in the form of an assertion and runs more or less through the whole culture. It is accepted by the society as true and valid, and as a rule is rarely questioned. Working together with other themes, it creates a distinct worldview that serves as a cognitive map for a society and shapes and guides the thinking and behavior patterns of its people. It is apparent and openly prompted by the society and manifests itself in both explicit and implicit ways.

Cultural Themes Illustrated

The following is a listing of cultural themes from six different types of cultures.[33] These themes will be used throughout the study to illustrate the various dimensions of cultural themes.

James Spradley and David McCurdy list five cultural themes found in the Apache culture, a closed and homogeneous culture.[34] (1) Men are physically, mentally, and morally superior to women. (2) The members of a kinship group share responsibility for what happens to each other. (3) Long life and old age are important goals. (4) Active participation in social life is required for authority and influence. (5) The universe is pervaded by supernatural powers accessible to any man or woman who desires to become a shaman.

Luzbetak presents four dominant themes common to the Middle Waghi tribal cultures of Papua New Guinea.[35] (1) The ultimate norm for good and bad is

---

[31] Luzbetak, 276.

[32] Spradley, *Interview*, 186.

[33] Many such examples are found in Kraft's discussion of these cultures in his preliminary draft to his book *Anthropology for Christian Witness*. These examples are not included in his 1997 edition. Charles H. Kraft, Anthropology for Christian Witness, vol. 2, unpublished manuscript, Fuller Theological Seminary, Pasadena, CA, 1994, 928-45.

[34] Spradley and McCurdy, *Anthropology*, 472-73.

[35] Luzbetak, 287-89.

the clan. (2) Security is found in the clan alone. (3) Successful living consists in the close cooperation among all members of the clan, living as well as departed and still unborn. (4) Man's most important material possession is the pig. Without the pig, native life would be impossible.

An example of cultural themes in a more complex and heterogeneous society is the themes associated with the American culture and the German culture. Thomas Williams lists four basic overriding themes underlying American culture.[36] (1) The universe is a mechanism. (2) Humans are masters of the universe. (3) All humans are equal. (4) Humans are perfectible.

Related to these primary themes, Kraft[37] and Luzbetak[38] list the following secondary themes. (a) Material prosperity and a high standard of living are signs of success. (b) Democracy, as discovered and perfected by the American people, is the ultimate form of living together. All men are created free and equal, and the United States has made this fact living reality. (c) Individual rights are to be respected and honored. (d) Judgments are to be made in dualist and polarizing terms that is something will be either / or, right / wrong, clean / dirty, good / bad, wise / stupid, work / play, with no middle gray area.

One of the major themes in German culture is *Ordnung* (order). It is a pursuit for order that has emerged out of an "angst" or fear of chaos and losing control. Maintaining order in the society is of utmost importance. David Marsh describes this theme as follows:

> The Germans fear society without order and organization; and so defer to older systems of guidance. This is the reason for an extraordinary lavishness to deep-seated principles of hierarchy, and to rules and regulations in general … They have perfected a system of economic and political [and social] consensus, which – partly because of worries about the consequences if a society ever became less organized – has become notoriously inflexible.[39]

Edward T. Hall shows how this theme affects the German society.

> Order is a dominant theme in German culture. In Germany there is order in all things. In handling space, Germans insist on well-defined, well-ordered territories with boundaries that are carefully protected since they

---

[36] Thomas Rhys Williams, *Introduction to Socialization* (St. Louis: C. V. Mosby, 1972), 225-26.

[37] Kraft, *Anthropology*, 940-41.

[38] Luzbetak, 277-78.

[39] David Marsh, *The Germans* (London: Century Hutchinson, 1989); quoted in Richard Hill, *We Europeans* (Brussels, Belgium: Europublications, 1992), 85, 88.

are very sensitive to spatial intrusion ... The sense of order reinforces a strong drive for conformity.[40]

Order based on "angst" (fear) has shaped every aspect of German society.

Paul Hiebert lists various cultural themes inherent in the modern western culture: (1) A split between spirit and matter, between subject and object, and therefore between subjective faith and objective truth; (2) a strong stress on order and a hierarchical view of life and society; (3) individualism and freedom; and (4) materialism.[41]

Finally, Scripture implies a possible cultural theme for the Jewish culture. From antiquity through the present, Jewish culture has centered on the observance of the Mosaic Law. John Bright points out that the law served as the central and integrating factor in New Testament Judaism around which all other cultural and religious structures and beliefs were organized. It provided Judaism with its distinct character. "The importance of the law in Judaism cannot be exaggerated."[42] Jesus' ministry on earth can only be understood fully in the context of this cultural theme.

The Origin of Cultural Themes

Culture and its cultural themes have their origin in God and are a gift from him to humanity. At the same time, they are a product of people's God-given creativity as they respond to the basic needs of life and its challenges. The 1983 Consultation of the World Evangelical Fellowship on the "Church in Response to Human Need" in Wheaton refers to this dual origin of culture.

> Culture [which includes cultural themes] is God's gift to human beings. God has made people everywhere in His image. As Creator, He has made us creative. This creativity produces culture ... Since every good gift is from above and since all wisdom and knowledge comes from Jesus Christ, whatever is good and beautiful in culture may be seen as a gift of God (James 1:16-18).[43]

Both origins are significant for this study.

---

[40] Edward T. Hall, *Understanding Cultural Differences: Keys to Success in West Germany, France, and the United States* (Yarmouth, ME: Intercultural Press, 1990), 43.

[41] Hiebert, "Gospel in Culture," 147-50.

[42] John Bright, *A History of Israel*, 3d ed. (Philadelphia: Westminster Press, 1981), 431-33.

[43] Scherer and Bevans, 286.

Cultural Themes: A Gift from God with a Redemptive Purpose

Cultural themes are a gift from God to man, which have a distinct purpose. They are part of God's creation and are designed to glorify him. Their ultimate purpose is to assist in the human-divine relationship. They are to bring people to God and to lead them to worship and glorify him.[44] Luzbetak alludes to this understanding of culture when he writes:

> They [cultures] must be viewed, rather, as systems of habits containing at least in some limited sense a 'hidden Christ', the result of God's own action and grace. The 'hidden Christ' is a force that the Church must look for, discover, and build upon. Evangelization should, in fact, be built on no other foundation than on the one that God himself in his universal love, providence, and mercy (c.f. 1 Tim. 4:7) has already laid. That foundation is most clearly visible in a people's culture – in their 'soul'.[45]

John Dawson's 'redemptive purpose' and Don Richardson's 'redemptive analogy' concepts are two possible ways of explaining the inherent purposes of cultural themes.

John Dawson's 'Redemptive Purpose'. Cultural themes have a redemptive purpose. In his book *Taking Our Cities for God*, John Dawson suggests that cities and social groupings have a redemptive gifting and a redemptive purpose.

> I believe our cities have the mark of God's sovereign purpose on them. Our cities contain what I call a redemptive gift. A city is a human institution, and like all institutions it develops a creative hand or personality that is greater than the sum of its parts. Each metropolis has unique characteristics when compared with other cities ... Any astute observer can see that certain cities seem to embody a cultural dream, and there is usually both a good and evil side to that dream. I believe God has participated in the creation of our cities both in forming their personality and in stationing high-ranking guardian angels over each one.[46]

---

[44] Wagner, "Visible and Invisible," 54.

[45] Luzbetak, 197.

[46] John Dawson, *Taking Our Cities for God* (Lake Mary, FL: Creation House, 1989), 39-40. Stephen Mansfield suggests that God's redemptive purpose and calling for Nashville is "to be a city of refuge in which people from every race and nation are sheltered, discipled, trained, and commissioned to proclaim the Gospel throughout the world," as well as "to be a center of Christian expression in the arts." Both vocations are closely associated with those themes that underlie all aspects of life in Nashville. Stephen Mansfield, "God's Redemptive Purpose for Nashville," in *Releasing Destiny*, ed. Stephen Mansfield (Nashville: Daniel 1 School of Leadership, 1993), 7-8.

What Dawson says about a city can also be applied to culture groups. Walter Wink refers to the redemptive purpose as a God-given vocation or calling.[47] Within each group, there is an inherent purpose or calling, which is often expressed through the cultural themes.

The Bible speaks of the purpose of the Jewish people. They are to be a light to other nations. The purpose of their dominant cultural theme, which is living by the law, is to point the Jews to the Messiah, and to serve as a light for the other nations (Rom. 7:7; 9:4-5; 11:11-12). The law was given to the Jewish nation with the purpose of bringing the nations to God through Jesus Christ.[48]

The redemptive purpose, vocation, and calling of a group is often found in one or more of its cultural themes. When looking at them, it is important to ask what God-given purpose the themes may possess or how they support the overall vocation and calling of a society.

Don Richardson's 'Redemptive Analogies'. Cultural themes also function as redemptive analogies.[49] This concept was developed by Don Richardson and states that there are various concepts or beliefs, which are held by a society and are waiting to be fulfilled. Redemptive analogies are the "catalyzing elements within a culture that anticipate aspects of the Gospel. Their God-ordained purpose is to precondition the minds to recognize Jesus as Savior."[50]

This concept may be expressed through a prophetic word, a statement of hope, folklore, or as is suggested here a cultural theme. Richardson proposes that these concepts have been placed there by God and serve as God's key to reaching humans in their culture. The analogies are vehicles or stepping-stones through which the gospel can enter or establish itself more naturally in the culture. Through the gospel message, the cultural concepts and themes find

---

[47] Wink, *Unmasking*, 93.

[48] For further discussion on Israel's redemptive purpose and calling, see Martin Buber, "The Gods of the Nations and God," in *Israel and the World* (New York: Schocken Books, 1948), 197-213; and Walter C. Kaiser Jr., "Israel's Missionary Call," in *Perspectives on the World Christian Movement: A Reader*, rev. ed., ed. Ralph D. Winter and Steven C. Hawthorne (Pasadena, CA: William Carey Library, 1992), A-25-33.

[49] Don Richardson, *Eternity in Their Hearts*, rev. ed. (Ventura, CA: Regal Books, 1984); *Peace Child* (Glendale, CA: Regal Books, 1974); and "Concept Fulfillment," in *Perspectives on the World Christian Movement: A Reader*, rev. ed., ed. Ralph D. Winter and Steven C. Hawthorne (Pasadena, CA: William Carey Library, 1992), C-59-63.

[50] Glossary in *Perspective on the World Christian Movement*, rev. ed., ed. Ralph D. Winter and Steven C. Hawthorne (Pasadena, CA: William Carey Library, 1992), E-10.

their fulfillment and their proper spiritual meaning and purpose.[51] Jesus stated, in relation to the Jewish theme of the law, that he did not come to abolish the law, but to fulfill it (Matt. 5:17).

An example of a cultural theme that functions as a redemptive analogy is the Navaho theme that "life is very, very dangerous." As a result of this theme, the society has taken precautions to deal adequately with the various perceived dangers. The gospel message provides a new and more effective way to deal with life's dangers. In Jesus Christ, the theme finds its proper understanding and fulfillment. Life is dangerous, but in Jesus Christ there is protection and guidance.

Dawson's 'redemptive purpose' and Richardson's 'redemptive analogy' are two examples of how the cultural theme's godly origin and purpose can be understood. Each society has a special purpose and calling, which are built into its cultural themes and worldview. Their primary purpose is to glorify God and to assist in God's overall mission of returning people to himself.

Cultural Themes: A Product of Human Creativity

Cultural themes are the result of humanity's God-given creativity. As a result, the various groups have developed different approaches to dealing with life's questions and challenges. Kraft elaborates on this idea:

> However impressive the array of common needs may be, we observe that since most of the problems we face are capable of different answers, different societies have radically different approaches to dealing with these needs and problems. Human beings are too creative to simply go about solving the same problems in the same ways. We develop different answers to the same problems and, over time, groups who prefer one set of approaches split off from groups that prefer another set of approaches. Then in isolation from each other, they move even more rapidly in different directions ... Because we are made in the image of God, we are able to develop creative approaches to problems and God seems to like creativity and diversity.[52]

The formation of these assumptions and themes are influenced, among other things, by the unique creativity of the people, their environment, the society's history, group decisions and alliances, as well as individual and corporate sins.[53] Together, under the leadership of God's guidance, these factors create

---

[51] Richardson, "Concept Fulfillment," C-60.

[52] Kraft, *Anthropology*, 120-21.

[53] Some view sin as the primary or even exclusive reason for the differences in culture. Even though sin plays a key role in the development of the themes, it is man's

and shape each culture's responses to the various challenges and needs of life, establishing its unique cultural themes and worldview.

The Functional Purpose of Cultural Themes

Through human creativity, each society has developed basic and unique assumptions, premises and cultural themes, which provide a starting point for explaining and perceiving the world around them and in dealing with the basic needs, questions, and challenges of life.

Worldview Universals.

Kraft lists five key areas of reality, which are addressed by all cultures.[54] They are called 'Worldview Universals' and are as follows: (1) Categorization deals with the way people categorize their perceptions. (2) Person-Group relationships address the way people relate to one another on an individual or group basis. (3) Causality provides a framework for explaining how things are caused and by whom. It answers questions like what causes things? What powers are responsible for a cause? What powers and forces are at work? Are the powers personal, impersonal, or both? (4) Time-Event looks at how time and events are perceived. (5) Space answers the questions of how humans conceive, arrange, and relate to space and material objects.

Cultural themes are the assumptions and premises, which provide the people direction in dealing with these universal issues. Some themes address only one of the universals, whereas the more dominant themes will attend to all five areas.

The Apache theme that "men are superior to women" provides a starting point and guiding principle in understanding and living out the relationship between the sexes. The Waghi theme that "the clan is the basis for what is right and wrong" provides the criteria for categorizing various behaviors. The Ashanti cultural theme that the gods and ancestral spirits control and direct the operation of all the forces of the universe, a common theme in many cultures, illustrates how themes answer the question of causality.

Basic Human Needs

Cultural themes also provide answers and give directions for meeting basic human needs. Charles Kraft has divided the basic needs into four categories:

---

creativity that is primarily responsible for the differences in cultures. The impact of sin will be discussed later in the chapter. Ibid., 120.

[54] Charles Kraft, *Christianity with Power* (Ann Arbor, MI: Vine Books, 1989), 195-205.

(1) Biological Needs include the need for food, air, health, shelter, sex, etc. (2) Psychological Needs refer to the need for meaning, for the maintenance of the individual psyche, to express oneself, etc. (3) Sociocultural Needs deal with the need for communication, providing for the transmission of culture, and maintenance of the social system. (4) Spiritual needs address the need for understanding and relating to supracultural beings and forces. Each cultural theme will provide the framework for dealing with these basic needs.

The Function of Cultural Themes

The cultural themes and their corresponding worldview fulfill a number of different functions. Some of the most important ones are:[55] (1) Explanation – Cultural themes lay the foundation for how a culture explains and deals with reality. It provides answers to the question of Who? What? When? How? Why? (2) Evaluation and Validation – The themes provide values, priorities, and goals for evaluating those matters and circumstances that affect an individual or a society. (3) Assigning and Prioritizing Commitments – Commitments, allegiances, and loyalties to people, institutions, things, values, and activities are determined by the themes. This function also determines the degree of importance and emotional attachment that is placed on the different allegiances and commitments. (4) Interpretation – Cultural themes interpret and assign meaning to all aspects of life. They decide what is or is not important. (5) Integration – The various aspects of culture are joined and held together by the themes to form a logically coherent framework for living. (6) Adaptation – The themes set up a framework for responding to new ideas and new experiences as well as for integrating them into the cultural matrix. They also provide the foundation for dealing with new elements, which stand in opposition to the existing worldview and its themes.

Cultural themes have both a descriptive and a prescriptive function. On the one hand, they mirror the values, ideals, and distinct characteristics of the society. The American theme of democracy describes the values and ideals held by a society. On the other hand, themes serve as the norms and standards of a society. The Waghi theme, which states that the clan is the ultimate norm for good and bad, provides the tribe with a standard for decision-making.

The Deep-Level Impact of Cultural Themes

These assumptions and cultural themes lie at the heart of a culture and impact the individual and his or her society on a cognitive, emotional, evaluative, and motivational level.[56] (1) The Cognitive Level – The cultural themes provide a

---

[55] Ibid., 181-93.

[56] Hiebert points out that culture in general relates to the ideas, feelings, and values of

starting point for the reasoning process and serve as a cognitive paradigm for the society.⁵⁷ (2) The Emotional Level – Themes impact the emotional life of a society. They influence the society's taste as well as feelings toward other people and life in general. The themes are usually associated with a deep, emotional reaction.⁵⁸ (3) The Evaluative Level – Cultural themes provide the foundation for the standards, norms, and values of a society. Cultural allegiances, right and wrong, truth and error, and important and unimportant matters are largely shaped and determined by the themes.⁵⁹ (4) The Motivational Level – The priorities, goals, and ideals of the society are established by the themes. They are the starting point and the motivating force for one's actions.⁶⁰

The cultural themes lie at the center of culture and impact how a society thinks, feels, evaluates, and motivates itself, as well as determine how a socie-

---

a society. He understands them as the basic dimensions of a culture and refers to them as the cognitive, affective, and evaluative dimensions. Luzbetak refers to them as the cognitive, emotional, and motivational dimensions. Hiebert's evaluative category and Luzbetak's motivational category are similar, yet differ enough to warrant two categories. The evaluative dimension deals with the values and norms of a society, whereas the motivational dimension focuses on the goals and driving force which lead to and bring about certain actions. For a more detailed discussion on these categories, see Hiebert, *Insights*, 39; and Luzbetak, 253-55.

⁵⁷ A common theme in many cultures is the belief in an interactive supernatural dimension. One of the Apache themes states that the universe is pervaded by supernatural powers and accessible through the shaman. Cause and effect is explained in supernatural terms. Reality is understood as an interplay between the supernatural and natural forces. The culture's reasoning process is significantly shaped by this view of reality. Kraft, "Christian Witness," unpublished manuscript, 939.

⁵⁸ Douglas Pennoyer's description of the cultural theme of the Tawbrid tribe in the Philippines shows the emotional dimension that is connected to the theme. "The interior Tawbrid are in a closed culture dominated by an awesome fear of strangers and even each other. Strangers are assumed to be kidnappers, disease carriers, or evil spirits. The people take elaborate precautions to avoid contact with anyone they do not recognize." Pennoyer, "Collective Captivity," 255.

⁵⁹ The theme that life is very, very dangerous has led the Navaho society to establish norms and values that respond to the theme. These include (1) maintain orderliness in those sectors of life which are little subject to human control, (2) be wary of non-relatives, (3) when in a new and dangerous situation, do nothing, and (5) escape. Spradley and McCurdy, 482-83.

⁶⁰ The foreign policy of the United States is conducted based on the theme that "democracy, as discovered and perfected by the American people, is the ultimate form of living together. All men are created free and equal, and the United States has made this fact a living reality." Kraft, "Christian Witness," 950.

ty deals with the worldview universals and life's basic needs. All the themes and assumptions put together create a society's worldview. This worldview then shapes and is shaped by the various structures and forms. The worldview interrelates and impacts the subsystems of religion, law, politics, aesthetics, technology, economics, social organizations, kinship, ideology, etc. to create a cohesive culture.

Major, Minor, and Counter Cultural-Themes

The worldviews are shaped by a number of different cultural themes. Within each culture there are major, dominant themes, as well as minor subthemes, which may be limited to one or more cultural subsystems. These major themes, also referred to as core themes, tend to be more influential, dominant, and visible than the minor themes. Their influence reaches into all areas of culture. The impact of the dominant American theme, all men are created equal, can be observed in the various subsystems of American culture, such as religion, social relationships, economics, law, technology, and politics. The more dominant a theme is the greater its influence and control will be on the society. In some cases, the themes are so dominant that they may appear to be the only relevant theme. However, the theory, proposed by Ruth Benedict, that there is only one defining theme for a culture, has been dismissed by most anthropologists.

Minor themes or subthemes function as corollaries to the major themes. Some minor themes often restate the major themes for a specific context or situations. The Waghi assumption that to disagree with one's clan is shameful and in some cases an act of treason is a subtheme of the dominant theme that the ultimate norm for right and wrong is the clan. Some minor themes are 'subsystem-specific-assumptions' that apply to and underlie a specific cultural subsystem or domain.[61] The importance of pigs in Waghi society is a theme that affects all areas of life, but its primary impact is in the area of economics.[62]

Opler points out that the significance and dominance of a theme can be measured by three indicators:[63] (1) The more frequent a theme is expressed in a society, the greater its significance. (2) The level of reaction that a theme receives when it is violated is a second indicator of its importance. Opler notes "the intensity of the reaction and the character of the sanctions involved are significant clues."[64] (3) Finally, the most telling indicator of a theme's domi-

---

[61] Kraft, *Anthropology*, 122.

[62] Luzbetak, 287-89.

[63] Opler, *Themes*, 200-1.

[64] Ibid., 200.

nance is the level of the constraints, which control the number, force, and variety of a theme's expressions. These constraints are called counter themes. The stronger the counter themes, the less significant and influential are the major themes.

The counter themes maintain a natural balance within the culture. Most dominant themes have a counter theme. The American theme that material prosperity and a high standard of living is a sign of success stands in contrast to the counter theme that "the kind of person you are is more important than how successful you are."[65] The interplay between dominant themes and counter themes plays a major role when introducing change into a society. Every society needs to maintain equilibrium. If a theme becomes too strong or is questioned, a culture tends to become unbalanced, leading to a modification of the existing themes and a restructuring of the corresponding worldview.

The Visible Manifestations of Cultural Themes

A society's cultural themes express themselves either in an explicit or implicit, primary or secondary, or in a formal or informal manner.[66] Explicit vehicles are visible, discernible, and direct manifestations of the theme. One of the most common vehicles of expression is folklore.[67] It includes myths, legends, fables, proverbs, riddles, and fairy tales. They explain and promote how things got the way they are and why they stay that way, as well as train the individual in how to think and reasons according to the culture's worldview and themes. Another significant vehicle is ritual. Hiebert states, that "People express their religious [as well as worldview] beliefs in creeds and stories and in ritual behavior. The study of these symbol systems can provide us with a great deal of insight into the ways people think and the ways they organize their culture."[68] Other expressions include mottoes, slogans, jokes, reoccurring expressions, common sayings, laws, expressed norms, rules, symbols, beliefs, as well as the arts.[69]

Themes may also become associated with individuals or fictional characters valued by the society. Often a local hero, mythical figure, or a folk hero will

---

[65] Kraft, *Anthropology*, 940-41.

[66] This discussion is based on Spradley's analysis of cultural-theme expressions. Spradley, *Interview*, 187.

[67] Kraft, *Anthropology*, 263-64.

[68] Hiebert, *Anthropology*, 372-76. For a discussion on myths and rituals in conjunction with worldview and themes, see Luzbetak, 266-76.

[69] The common saying that "There is a Policeman in every German" or "Ordnung muß sein" are examples of the German theme of *Ordnung*.

embody the ideals and themes of a society. Comic book and movie heroes in the United States (e.g., Superman, Batman, Indiana Jones, etc.) are often rugged individualists, heralding individualism as the highest ideal.

In many instances, the theme's expression has become institutionalized. In some cases, the institution becomes structured around a central theme. Occasionally the theme becomes so closely associated with the institution that they become synonymous. Wall Street embodies the American theme that material prosperity and a high standard of living are signs of success. Often the validity and influence of the theme is so closely tied to the vehicle that its existence is dependent on the vehicle itself.

In most cases, the cultural themes are the implicit, unspoken force that underlies the various visible forms, products, and actions of a culture. People are subconsciously aware of the themes, rely on them to organize their lives, but find it difficult to express the theme in words.

Luzbetak suggests that themes are further expressed through primary or secondary means of communication. Certain behavior or events express the content of the theme in a direct manner. The Apache theme that men are superior to women, for instance, is expressed in that men precede women while walking and eating. The secondary means are implied or symbolic expressions of the theme. Events are often judged and interpreted based on the theme. In the Apache culture, the excessive movement of a baby in a womb is a sign that the baby is a boy because excessive movement indicates strength and superiority.[70]

The vehicles of expression can either be formal or informal. Formalized vehicles express the themes in a regulated manner. Society insists that the expressed themes are obeyed and followed. Formal vehicles include rules, laws, or rituals. Unformalized vehicles are less strict and include norms, expectations, and mottoes, which advocate adherence indirectly and through persuasion.[71] Knowing the nature of the theme's manifestation and the vehicles through which it is expressed are important in order to bring about successful change to the themes.

Summary

Cultural themes lie at the heart of the culture and shape the society and its culture. They are basic, unchallenged, and interrelated assumptions and premises dealing with reality and the various aspects of life, which run through all

---

[70] Luzbetak, 277.
[71] Ibid.

parts of a culture. They shape and organize the society's cultural matrix and function as a guide and map for the society. The themes impact the cognitive, emotional, evaluative, and motivational dimensions. The various themes combined make up a society's worldview.

The themes have a functional purpose as well as a spiritual one. The themes provide a basis for dealing with life's questions, problems, and challenges. Many of the themes also serve spiritual functions. They can express God's redemptive gift for the society or act as redemptive analogies, providing an entrance for the gospel into the society.

The number of themes and their importance vary. The more dominant a theme becomes in a society, the more influence it has. Each major theme has a counter theme that keeps the culture in balance. Because of the themes' nature, purpose, and function, they are able to exert a tremendous amount of influence over the individuals of a society.

Finally, the themes can be expressed explicitly and implicitly, through primary and secondary means, as well as through formal and informal vehicles of communication. Some expressions are direct while other infers the presence of a cultural theme. In some cases, the theme becomes synonymous with the vehicle of expression. The vehicles are the basis for dealing with and transforming the themes.

The Impact of Cultural Themes on Individuals and Their Society

The influence of cultural themes on the group as a whole and its individuals are deep rooted, extensive, and far-reaching. They function to a large degree as a dynamic system of control for the society. In order to analyze the nature of the cultural themes' influence, it is important to understand the types of groups and societies in which they exist. This will be followed by an analysis of the nature and means of the cultural themes' influence.

The Nature of "People Groups"

Every human being belongs to a number of different groups and social networks through either formal or informal membership, birth, race, nationality or other common characteristics. Each of these different societies and groups functions around shared themes, which shape and condition the views, values, norms, and behavior of the group. The themes' level of influence on the individual is determined by the nature of the group as well as the degree of one's association and enculturation into the group.

A Definition of "People Group"

Edward Dayton and David Fraser define a group of people ('People Group') who share a common culture as

> a collection of humans who see themselves (or are seen by others) as culturally distinct from other groups. They share certain cultural traits such as language, religion, values, and often a common history. Usually there is a degree of pride associated with the life-style of the group. Members feel that their way of life is right for them and is better than the customs and ideas held by other groups. Usually they wish to cultivate the cultural elements which they see as important and to pass them on to the next generation ... and who perceive to have a common affinity for one another.[72]

Geography often plays an important role in the perceived identity of the group. The group may or may not be defined by its geographic boundaries. Even though geography is important, it should not be the main criterion for defining a group. A 'people group' is defined primarily by its common traits and the perceived identity of its members.

There are a number of classifications for groups. They can be classified according to size, openness, relationship to other groups, rites of membership, geography, common affinities, kinship, race, etc. This section will look at two factors that are relevant to the study of cultural themes: size, commonly perceived identity, and common characteristics.

Classification According to the Size of the Group

Kraft breaks down groups by their sizes and their relationship to one another.[73] He refers to them as cultures or subcultures. He lists the groups from the smallest to the broadest. (1) The personal culture – Each person has a unique personal culture and personal themes, which shape his or her life. (2) The family culture or smaller subcultures – These include the extended family, clans, gangs, groups of friends, etc. (3) Community cultures – These include voluntary associations and societal groups on a local level. (4) Regional cultures, e.g., the Southern culture, the Navaho, or Apache culture. (5) National cultures, e.g., the American or German culture. (6) Multinational cultures, e.g., the Western culture or Asian culture. Each individual will belong to one or more cultures on each of these levels.

---

[72] Dayton and Fraser, 132-36.
[73] Kraft, *Anthropology*, 40.

The larger the group and the more involuntary one's association is to the culture, the more implicit and deep rooted the influence of cultural themes will be on an individual and the harder it will be to make any changes to the themes. The smaller and more limited the cultures are, the more aware the people are of the themes and the more apparent and stronger their influence will be. However, in contrast to the themes of the larger groups, these themes are easier to detect and to deal with. The size of the group influences how one deals with the themes.

Classification According to the Commonly Perceived Identity of the Group

Groups can also be classified according to the way people relate to the group and perceive the group identity. Robert Bierstedt has identified four types of groups according to this criterion.[74] These include statistical groups,[75] societal groups, social groups, and associations. Cultural themes are common in the last three groups.

Societal Groups

These groups share a common identity. Hiebert states, "societal groups are the mental categories by which people sort out themselves and other human beings on the basis of similarity of kind."[76] There is an awareness of "we-ness" based on common visible signs (e.g., age, sex, race, etc.), distinctive traits (e.g., language, customs, traditions, common beliefs, religion, etc.), or sociological distinctives (e.g., heritage, geography, ethnic differences, social classes, etc.). The group awareness provides these groups with a common culture and distinct cultural themes.

Social Groups

Social groups also share a common identity, but in contrast to societal groups, they are also defined by the networks of interaction that exist among their

---

[74] See Robert Bierstedt, *The Social Order*, 3d ed. (New York: McGraw-Hill, 1970), 272-301, for a more detailed discussion. Dayton and Fraser as well as Hiebert provide an overview of this classification of groups. Dayton and Fraser, 133-35; and Hiebert, *Anthropology*, 178-80.

[75] Statistical groups are based on demographic statistics. They are defined on the basis of certain characteristics that individuals share in common. Common geography, nationality, income, race, likes and dislikes, etc. These groups are usually created for the sake of analysis, and the people in the groups are usually unaware of their existence. The group is held together by an artificial criterion and usually does not have a common culture or shared cultural themes.

[76] Hiebert, *Anthropology*, 179.

members based on common beliefs, values, norms, and goals. These groups include families, friendships, congregations, neighborhoods, clans, etc. The members have a high degree of self-identity as well as allegiance and loyalty to the group. Often social groups will develop within societal groups and become subcultures. The organization of the social group can be informal and unstructured, as well as formal and structured. It is within the context of the social groups that cultural themes have the greatest impact on the individual. Dayton and Fraser state that

> this group [social group] is most important in the formation of personality and culture and it's passing on from one generation to another. This is where people learn to conform to a relatively uniform set of customs and values. This is the group that people consult when they are in the process of making a decision.[77]

Associations

These are formal groups that are structured and organized around common pursuits, goals, interests, or needs, which function in the group as cultural themes. They underlie and determine the norms, values, rules, activities, and membership requirements of the group. Associations may include special interest groups, churches, secret societies, gangs, companies, etc. These groups play an important role in modern societies, and in many cases their themes exert a significant, visible level of control over their members.

Cultural themes have usually been associated with larger ethnic and national cultures and societies. However, based on this study's understanding of cultural themes and people groups, the concept of cultural themes can appear in various kinds of groups. They are present in families, churches, associations, cliques, gangs, communities, ethnic groups, regional cultures, nations, and multinational groupings. The principles surrounding cultural themes, which have and will be presented in this and the following chapters can be applied to any group that has a common identity and shares a common culture.

The Nature of the Cultural Theme's Influence

Cultural Patterns Versus Cultural Performance

How do cultural themes influence individuals and the group as a whole? First, it is important to differentiate between cultural themes as structures and the

---

[77] Dayton and Fraser, 135.

use of the themes by the members of the group. Kraft refers to them as "cultural patterns" and "cultural performance".[78]

The "cultural patterns" are the structures, forms, and cultural components, including cultural themes that make up the cultural matrix. Kraft defines it as

> that enormously complex cultural grid into which we are indoctrinated before we realize what is happening to us ... What this patterning, or press, provides for the members of a culture is an extremely large number of rules, or boundaries, with reference to which they must operate.[79]

"Cultural performance," focuses on the group or individual's adoption of the cultural patterns to various life situations. "In our use of the cultural patterning (our performance), we both follow and alter the culture that we receive."[80]

There are those who believe that the "cultural patterns" themselves are responsible for the behavior of the individual. They view cultures as "an enormously powerful being that molds and pushes people around, determining or at least strongly influencing their beliefs and behavior, sometimes helpfully, sometimes harmfully." It is considered a "living organism, existing independently of those who practice it, with great power to influence their lives."[81]

In contrast, others like Kraft hold the view that the influence of culture is a result of the "cultural performance". Culture does not contain any power in and of itself. Kraft explains,

> Culture is not a person. It does not "do" anything. Only people do things. The fact that people ordinarily do what they do by following cultural "tracts" laid down for them should not lead us to treat culture itself as something possessing a life of its own. Culture is like a script an actor uses. He follows it most of the time ... The "power" that keeps people following the script of their culture is the power of habit, not any power that culture possesses in itself ... Cultural (including worldview) patterns, then, do not force people to follow them.[82]

---

[78] Kraft, *Christianity in Culture*, 69-70. Sherwood Lingenfelter makes the same differentiation, but refers to them as "the cultural system" and "the sociocultural level". Sherwood Lingenfelter, *Transforming Culture* (Grand Rapids: Baker Books, 1992), 204.

[79] Kraft, *Christianity in Culture*, 70.

[80] Ibid.

[81] Kraft, *Anthropology*, 36. This position is referred to as "cultural superorganicism."

[82] Kraft, *Christianity with Power*, 56-57.

Both views try to account for the tremendous influence culture and its themes have on people. Even though one is inclined to see culture as an independent powerful construct, it seems more reasonable to locate the source of culture's power in the individual's use of as well as his or her response to the cultural patterns. The more the cultural system and its patterns are integrated in a person's life, the greater impact the culture has on the individual.

In light of this understanding of culture, it can be concluded that cultural themes do not in and of themselves have the power to influence people. It is through the habitual use and reference to cultural themes that the themes exert and maintain control over a society and its individuals.

Habit: The Cultural Theme's Power Source

Culture and its themes are empowered and sustained by the force of habit. Kraft explains:

> Humans are creatures of habit. We do things in certain ways not simply because we have been taught to do them in those ways, but because we have gotten into the habit of doing them in certain ways. Worldview structuring provides the patterns, and those who are significant in our lives provide the modeling from which we learn the patterns, usually quite unconsciously. Most of these patterns we adopt and "habituate" with or without modification. Some of what is modeled or explained we reject. Not much of what we learn in our early years is rejected, however. It is largely assimilated at the unconscious level and practiced automatically without our being conscious of the presence of the patterns and habits that keep us following cultural tracks.[83]

In most cases, the habits surrounding the cultural themes are not questioned, have strong emotional ties, and are maintained by a deep-rooted commitment and allegiance. The habit itself is formed through the enculturation process and is sustained through society's set of social controls.

Enculturation: The Learning of Cultural Themes

Culture and its themes are consciously and subconsciously learned through enculturation. It is the process of becoming competent in one's culture. It teaches, establishes, engrains, and automatizes the cultural themes and related patterns and thus conditions one's thinking and behavior. The process is detailed and persuasive, deeply affecting a person's cognitive, emotional, evaluative, and motivational dimension. The themes and patterns become second nature. Luzbetak describes it as follows:

---

[83] Ibid., 58.

We are endlessly learning the way to do things, the way to speak and to feel and to think. Before long, we master our lesson so well that to think, speak, feel, or act in any other way will require effort and considerable violence to self to go contrary to the "proper" way. Culture thus becomes a kind of second nature to us, affecting our behavior and influencing our personality.[84]

The conditioning process is so effective that, as Kraft points out, "we are 100 percent culturally conditioned."[85]

This does not mean that the individual is culturally determined, a passive victim of the enculturation process. The individual is always free to choose to follow, resist or change the prescribed themes. Luzbetak points out that individuals are not "automatons". They "are largely molded by culture and are constantly pressured by it, but never are they shackled to it."[86] In some cultures, there is a greater freedom to pursue alternative ways, whereas in other cultures adherence to the themes is more strictly enforced.

Even though a society is not tied to their cultural themes, their implicit nature, their sweeping influence on the cultural matrix of a society, and their deep-rooted integration into the life of the individual and the society make it difficult to oppose or deviate from their prescribed path and close to impossible to escape from their influence. Cultural themes can become strongholds. The more dominant a theme becomes, the more likely it will turn into a cultural stronghold, which holds the individual and the society captive to a set pattern of thinking and behaving. The various cultural structures and related themes help strengthen the theme stronghold, and the social controls of the culture help maintain the dominance of the theme. The stronger and more dominant the themes become, the harder it is to escape their controlling grip.

The Press and Pull of Culture: The Control Mechanism of Cultural Themes

Enculturation establishes cultural themes, whereas the various social controls that maintain and strengthen the presence of the themes. The social control is a combination of the press and pull forces within the society. Kraft observes: "As humans, we seem to know intuitively that if the structures are to be preserved, they must be obeyed. People therefore attempt, with varying degrees of success, to press and pull each other into conformity to these structures."[87]

---

[84] Luzbetak, 186.
[85] Kraft, *Anthropology*, 150.
[86] Luzbetak, 188.
[87] Kraft, *Anthropology*, 154.

Cultural Press

Cultural press is the formal and informal pressures a society places on an individual to conform to the cultural pattern. Individuals tend not only to conform to the cultural norms and uphold their prescribed values, but insist that others observe them as well. Various forms of pressures are set up to ensure their compliance. Some of the more common pressures include the threat of physical and social punishment, fines, imprisonment, exile, gossip, shame, guilt, ridicule, threats and fear, scolding, laws and legal norms, and the fear of legal or spiritual reciprocity.[88] They function to pressure the society as a whole to conform to the prescribed ways. The form and severity of social controls produced through pressure vary from society to society.

Luzbetak describes the effect of the cultural press on a society as follows:

> Other things being equal, the more forceful and effective the social controls, the more persistent the culture. Aspects of culture to which little or no pressure is applied will tend to change more readily than those to which are attached severe and effective sanctions.[89]

Cultural Pull

Cultural pull draws the individual into following the cultural pattern by example and persuasion. This occurs through cultural heroes, role models, various forms of education, rewards for good behavior, logic, the prospect of prestige and admiration, praise, as well as various forms of advertising.[90] Cultural pull is the more common form of social control used in complex and open societies.

Cultural themes are maintained through the pulls and presses of a society. Depending on the size, nature, and complexity of the society, either the press or pull is more prevalent. It is important to remember that it is not the themes that press or pull the individual into conforming to the themes, but human beings and their institutions that exert the pull and press forces. Which people exercise control in a society? How do they use cultural themes to implement social controls?

---

[88] In many cultures, social pressures are effectively enforced through the fear of reciprocity from the spirit world. The individuals are pressed into a certain behavior, fearing that they will be cursed by or lose favor with the gods or spirits, if they do not conform. For a detailed description of this and other forms of cultural pressures, see Luzbetak, 356-57 and Kraft, *Anthropology*, 343-54.

[89] Luzbetak, 333.

[90] Ibid., 357.

Cultural Gatekeepers

A Definition

Every society has certain individuals who have influence and power over others. In most cases they are the implementers of the various social controls. They reinforce the cultural values, norms, standards, and cultural themes; shape opinions; model culturally approved or in some cases culturally deviant behavior; and influence the thinking and behavior of the people. Luzbetak refers to them as "powerhouses" of the society.[91] Kraft calls them "opinion leaders".[92]

This study will use the term "cultural gatekeepers", because one of the key functions of a gatekeeper in a society is to act as guardian and gatekeeper of the culturally approved ways. This study defines cultural gatekeepers as individuals, groups of people, or institutions that have a certain amount of influence over a segment of society and who communicate, integrate, and see to it that the culture with its norms, values, and core cultural themes is established and maintained through their influence.

The gatekeepers' power varies according to the nature of their group as well as the level of authority attributed to them. Some employ rigid and formal means, whereas others exert their influence in a more casual and informal manner. Some work through cultural press mechanisms, while others rely more on cultural pull tactics.

David Hesselgrave identifies two types of cultural gatekeepers with two types of influences. He differentiates between 'formal leaders' and 'opinion leaders' who possess either 'prestige influence' or 'personal influence'.[93]

Formal leaders have authority based on the position or title they hold and lead based on 'prestige influence'. Their power is associated with established cultural structures, such as political office or socially approved leadership positions (e.g., teachers, professors, religious leaders, etc.). Formal leaders tend to function as cultural gatekeepers more often than opinion leaders. However, their influence and persuasiveness is not as strong as those of the opinion leaders.

Opinion leaders are informal leaders who possess 'personal influence'. Hesselgrave defines this type of leadership as follows:

---

[91] Ibid., 358-59.

[92] Kraft, *Anthropology*, 374.

[93] David J. Hesselgrave, *Communicating Christ Cross-Culturally* (Grand Rapids: Zondervan Pub., 1991), 468.

> Personal influence is the product of access to information and also of personal characteristics such as force of personality, competency, and communication ability. It is more or less independent of one's position in the hierarchical ranking of the society and is usually exerted through face-to-face contacts.[94]

Opinion leaders usually do not hold an official position. Those who function as cultural gatekeepers usually represent and promote only one or two distinct themes. Their influence may also be limited to certain cultural domains (e.g., religion, medicine, politics, etc.). Their power of persuasion and influence are stronger than those of the formal leaders. In many societies and groups, the true power lies with the opinion leaders. Often these leaders are in the background and not readily detected. Cultural themes associated with opinion leaders are more deeply rooted and followed than those associated with formal leaders. When the opinion leadership and formal leadership are united into one person, the power of influence and level of control are significantly increased. This usually leads to some form of dictatorship (e.g., Hitler in Germany).

Cultural gatekeepers are usually associated with individuals. They include family heads, political leaders, sports heroes, movie stars, political advisors, outgoing charismatic leaders, respected elders in the community, or teenage idols. In some cases, the cultural gatekeepers are cultural institutions such as corporations (e.g., McDonalds or Disney Corporation), government institutions (e.g., court systems), or leadership forums. Even though a leadership team runs the power in these organizations, the institution can take on a life of its own whose power of influence supersedes that of its leadership. The leadership merely maintains the message and cultural themes that have come to be associated with the institutions.

Cultural Gatekeepers and Cultural Themes

The cultural gatekeepers either implements, maintain, or express the cultural theme through their persona, their influence, or their use of the themes to influence people.

(1) Cultural gatekeepers become associated with cultural themes. In some cases the themes are associated with the persons themselves, in other cases they become associated with the position the gatekeeper holds. The gatekeepers model the cultural theme in their behavior and leadership. This is the situation with cultural heroes, who exemplify the cultural ideals as established through the themes. The cultural theme is integrated into the lives of people as they admire and follow the gatekeepers' lead.

---

[94] Ibid.

(2) The cultural gatekeeper becomes the administrator of the cultural theme. He interprets, implements, maintains, and ensures that the people follow and maintain the themes. This is especially the case for themes that deal with cultural values and morality. The Waghi leadership is responsible for interpreting, implementing, and enforcing the theme that the ultimate norm of good and bad is the clan. In New Testament Judaism, the Pharisees and Sadducees were the protectors and enforcers of the Mosaic Law.

(3) Cultural themes provide the gatekeeper with his or her power of influence. The cultural theme that the spirit world directs and controls the universe gives the local shaman or religious leader, who serve as mediator between the spirit world and the people, his or her power of influence. The stronger the belief is in the theme, the stronger the influence of the gatekeeper.

When working with cultural themes and analyzing the nature of their influence, one must consider the cultural gatekeepers. Through their presence, cultural themes are integrated and maintained in a society. Any attempt to bring about change or alter the themes will need to identify and deal with the cultural gatekeepers.

Summary

Cultural themes have an enormous and significant influence over the society and its people. The themes do not have power in themselves but gain their power by people subjecting to, conforming to, and upholding their directives. The influencing power of themes comes through the human propensity to live by habit. Through learning and integrating the various themes on a cognitive, emotional, evaluative, and motivational level, the themes condition and shape the thinking and behavior patterns of the individual. A deep-rooted allegiance to the themes is established through the enculturation process and maintained through various cultural pressures and pull forces. When the themes become excessively dominant, they can create a cultural stronghold centered on the themes.

Cultural gatekeepers ensure that people conform to the themes and that they are properly upheld. The gatekeepers are either individuals or institutions, which have some degree of influence over a segment of society, either through their position or their personal character and persuasiveness. Any attempt to deal with or transform the themes will need to deal with the gatekeepers.

Even though the cultural themes exert a tremendous amount of influence over people, they are not static or determinative. Cultural themes are able to change, and people are able to choose to conform or not conform to the themes.

The Impact of Sin on Cultural Themes

In light of the fact that cultural themes have a significant influence on a society, it is important to raise the question regarding the basic character of the themes. Are the themes in their essence good, neutral, or corrupt? This section will look at the effect sin has on the basic nature, content, expression, and use of cultural themes and how this has influenced its use as a missiological tool. This section will provide the basis for understanding the influence, which demonic powers have on the cultural themes.

The Basic Disposition of Culture Themes

Are cultures and their cultural themes inherently good, neutral, or corrupt? There are three basic positions on this issue.[95]

(1) Culture is inherently corrupted through sin. This view is referred to as the 'low level' of culture. Richard Niebuhr has labeled it 'the God-against-culture' position. Culture is equated with the concept of the "world" as found in 1 John 2:15-16. The "world" is understood as inherently corrupt and under the control of Satan's power. It is therefore assumed that the essence of culture is evil. Christians are called "to not be of this world" which is interpreted to mean one should withdraw, reject, escape, or insulate him or her from culture's influence.

Even though this position takes the presence of evil seriously, it fails to understand adequately the concept of culture. Culture is not external, but it is part of the person's composition. Even though it is possible to transform, change, replace, and alter one's culture, it is impossible to be without culture or to escape its influence. This position further assumes that culture is under the complete control of Satan and, therefore, is completely evil. Even though some aspects of culture may be corrupt or be used for evil purposes, many aspects of culture are still fulfilling their intended purpose.

Many proponents of this position believe there is a uniform Christian culture, which is endorsed by God, is built on biblical teachings, and functions as the one true culture. Those who hold this view suggest that there are God-ordained forms, structures, and themes, which form the ideal culture. It is referred to as the "Christian culture" or the "biblical culture." Christians are to turn from the worldly cultures to this Christian culture. This position fails to realize that the Christ-likeness of a culture is not measured by its forms and

---

[95] This arrangement is based on both Charles Kraft's and Richard Niebuhr's classification. Kraft, *Christianity in Culture*, 103-11; and H. Richard Niebuhr, *Christ and Culture* (New York: Harper & Row, 1951).

structures, but in how these forms are applied. In most cases, the various proposed "Christian cultures" are nothing more than one's own worldly culture shaped by biblical principles, teaching, and forms.[96]

According to this position, a culture's themes are considered for the most part to be corrupted assumptions, which have no redeeming value. As a Christian, one needs to free himself from their influence and turn to the new set of Christian cultural themes.

(2) Culture is in its essence good. Culture and its themes are considered inherently good. This position is also known as the 'high view' of culture or the 'Christ-in-culture' approach. It views culture and its components as good, properly fulfilling their functional and God-given purpose. They do not need to be changed by the gospel. This position is based on a high respect for the people and their unique cultural heritage. As a result, the gospel is often accommodated to fit the cultural forms and structures without adequate critical evaluation.[97] The evils of society are exclusively associated with the individuals, not with the cultural structures.

The major weakness of this view is that it does not take the impact of corporate and individual sin seriously enough. It maintains a naive view of culture and sin, which can lead to syncretistic tendencies. Charles Kraft, who previously held this view, points out its flaws.

> With these assumptions, we often completely ignored the kinds of influences the enemy wields through people and their culture ... we often neglected the fact that structures created by humans under Satan's influence are unlikely to be either totally neutral or easily usable for God's purposes.[98]

It is important to note that the gospel calls not only people to change, but societies and their cultures as well.[99] This position was favored by many anthropologically trained missionaries of the 1960s and 1970s in response to the 'low-view' of culture, which had prevailed in missions until recently.[100]

---

[96] Kraft, *Christianity in Culture*, 108.
[97] Hiebert, *Insights*, 185.
[98] Kraft, *Anthropology*, 451.
[99] Hiebert, *Insights*, 185.
[100] The 'low view' of culture was the predominant position held by those from the early missionary movement. Their goal was to lead people away from their native culture to a western, civilized culture (viewed as the Christianized culture) in order to evangelize them. Kraft, *Anthropology*, 451.

(3) Culture is inherently neutral and can be used for good or evil purposes. The third position views culture as neutral, which has a good and useful purpose, yet has been perverted by sin and is in need of transformation. This position is similar to Charles Kraft's 'God-above-but-through-culture', approach, Paul Hiebert's 'critical contextualization' approach, and Richard Niebuhr's 'transformation' or 'conversionists' approach. The key premise is that culture in its original state is neutral, but has been influenced by human sinfulness and has fallen under the control of Satan. "Culture, therefore, is seen as corrupted but convertible, usable, perhaps even redeemable by God's grace and power. Culture is perverted but not evil in essence."[101] It is in need of redemption and transformation. The goal is to return the various structures of culture to their intended purposes.

In contrast to the 'low view' of culture, the third position holds a more positive view of culture. In most cases, the sin-influenced culture still adequately serves humanity in its intended functional purpose. In contrast to the second position, the presence of sin is taken more seriously. Culture and its structures can promote the divine-human relationship or oppose it. In many cases, the corrupted structures and themes function as a barrier to the gospel, hindering the divine-human relationship. The criterion for evaluating cultural themes and other structures is their compliance to biblical principles.

This last position shows the two different ways cultural themes relate to the gospel message. On one hand, the themes provide adequate and biblically sound answers to life's questions and serve as tools for the advancement of the gospel. On the other hand, the themes become distorted through sinful influences so that they either directly oppose the gospel message or they create ungodly and destructive structures which oppose the gospel and its messengers. Because of the basic nature of themes, the themes should neither be rejected nor uncritically accepted, but should be critically evaluated based on biblical principles and transformed to their original meaning and purpose when needed.

The Extent of Sin's Influence on Cultural Themes

There are two views concerning the degree to which sin influences culture and its cultural themes. Kraft believes sin affects cultural themes in its content, its expression, and its use by the society. It does not affect the concept of culture nor that of cultural themes, which both remain neutral in their essence. Kraft elaborates:

---

[101] Kraft, *Christianity in Culture*, 113.

> I see cultural structuring, ... as basically a vehicle or milieu, neutral in essence, though warped by the pervasive influence of human sinfulness. Culture is not in and of itself either an enemy or a friend to God or humans. It is, rather, something that is there to be used by personal beings such as humans, God, and Satan ... Human beings, however, are pervasively infected by sin. This means that the ways in which humans use the cultural forms, patterns, and processes at their disposal are always affected by sin. The meanings intended and the meanings received are likewise tainted by the ways in which humans use their cultures. Apparently no human motive is unaffected by sin. Therefore, no aspect of culture is used by human beings with pure intent ... It is the use of the cultural structures that is changeable (at least at first), not usually the structures themselves.[102]

The term "neutral" refers to the forms and functions of the culture. "Cultural patterning, organizing, and structuring of life, the functions they are intended to serve, and the processes cultures make available to human beings are not seen as inherently evil or good themselves."[103]

In contrast to Kraft, Sherwood Lingenfelter views culture and cultural themes not only as structures affected by sin in its content, expression, and use, but also evil in its basic nature. Culture and cultural themes, in their essence, can and do oppose the gospel and serve as a prison of disobedience. Lingenfelter states that "these social systems and world views become prisons of disobedience, entangling those who hold them in a life of conformity to social images that at their roots are in conflict with God's purpose for humanity as expressed in Jesus Christ."[104]

Lingenfelter rejects Kraft's basic assumption that culture is still neutral and compares culture to a slot machine that is programmed to promote corrupt power structures and forces. "The structures and organizations of culture are not neutral; people define and structure their relationships with others to protect their personal or group interests, and to sustain or gain advantage over others with whom they compete."[105]

Even though Lingenfelter and Kraft disagree as to the nature of sin's influence, both agree that culture-change needs to occur foremost through a change within people.

---

[102] Ibid., 113-14.

[103] Ibid.

[104] Lingenfelter, 17.

[105] Ibid., 18.

> Transformation is neither bridging from one system to another, nor transferring a "Christian" system to another place and people. Rather, transformation means a new hermeneutic – a redefinition, a reintegration of the lives of God's people (the church) within the system in which they find themselves living and working.[106]

Through the change in the individual, "the Gospel may become a significant powerful force in the continuous restructuring of any social environment and worldview."[107]

Since the effects of sin are deeply ingrained in culture, as Lingenfelter points out, it is more reasonable to view the concept of cultural themes as neutral, which become affected by sin through human interaction. There is nothing inherently wrong, destructive, or sinful in seeking answers and establishing structures to deal with the basic questions and needs of life, nor is there anything inherently sinful in establishing a plan or strategy for living. Cultural themes as a concept is neither good nor evil. The content, expressions, and use of the themes, on the other hand, can and will display the effects of sin because they are partially an expression of man's creativity, which is affected by sin.

It is important to differentiate here between form and meaning. The cultural theme as a form is neutral. However, the meaning and content associated with the themes and their use are subject to sin and its influence. It is true that some structures and forms in their essence are more likely to establish a godly content, whereas others may have a tendency to be used for more destructive purposes, but this does not constitute a sinful or destructive nature as such.

The Apache theme that men are superior to women deals with the relationship between the sexes. The need to provide a proper premise for the relationship between the sexes is not sinful in itself. However, the way this relationship is conceived and projected throughout one's culture can be in conflict with the biblical understanding of the relationship, as seems to be the case in the Apache culture.

Cultural themes are in their essence neutral, and can be used for godly or corrupt purposes. When dealing with cultural themes and their impact on people, the focus should not be on the structure of cultural themes, but on their content, expression, and use. Change does not seek a structural change, but a transformation of the theme's content, expression, and use. Cultural themes should not be rejected or eliminated, but should be transformed to correspond

---

[106] Ibid., 19.
[107] Ibid., 20.

to biblical principles and Scripture's view of reality. This concept will be further developed in chapter 5.

The Nature of Sin's Influence on Cultural Themes

The Effects of the Human Fall

When humanity rebelled and sinned against God, all of creation, including culture and its themes, became corrupted by sin. The 1983 statement by the World Evangelical Fellowship on the "Church in Response to Human Need" states that

> Culture is God's gift to human beings ... However, people have sinned by rebelling against God. Therefore the cultures we produce are infected with evil. Different aspects of our culture show plainly our separation from God. Social structures and relationships, art forms and laws often reflect our violence, our sense of lostness, and our loss of coherent moral values.[108]

Sin is "missing the mark" by failing to live up to God's standards and purposes. As a result of man's sin, that which is good becomes perverted and distorted.[109] This perversion also affects the cultural themes. Many of them become distorted and are no longer able to live up fully to God's standards and their God-given purpose. They usually deviate in some degree from or contradict biblical principles and values. They are a reflection of man's rebellious and sinful nature.

In other cases, the sin-tainted themes give the society a distorted base for dealing with life's questions and needs. As a result, the basic issues of life are treated in a context that is outside of God's revelation and the human-divine relationship. Hesselgrave states it this way:

> One of the disastrous aspects of man's sin was that he did not retain God in his knowledge. As a result man's understanding has been perverted in precisely those areas where divine revelation is crystal clear. The true God is excluded, but false gods abound. Men distinguish between good and evil in some way, but not in accordance with the biblical view.[110]

---

[108] Scherer and Bevans, 286.

[109] Perversion is the act of turning someone or something away from the right path. Distortion is twisting and misrepresenting the original meaning and purpose of something.

[110] Hesselgrave, 150.

This does not mean that all cultural themes are distorted and useless. Some reflect a clear view of reality whereas others express a somewhat distorted, yet adequate view. Most cultural themes fall into this last category. Some themes are perverted and distorted to such an extent that their content and use stand in direct opposition to the gospel message. They keep a society in bondage to ideas, traditions, perceptions, behavior patterns, and alliances that separate them from the life-bringing gospel and support and perpetuate destructive ideas, power structures, and behavior.

The more dominant the sin-distorted themes are in a culture, the stronger the effects of the distortion are on the society. Once the distorted themes become a major dominant theme in a society, it becomes a stronghold, which opposes the gospel. The degree to which cultural themes are distorted by sin determines the positive or negative effect the theme has missions.

The Waghi theme that good and bad is determined by what is best for the tribe illustrates how a distorted theme operates. It fulfills its proper function in the society, providing it with an effective criterion for evaluating. Yet this criterion is in conflict with biblical teaching and most likely will be a hindrance for the gospel message. This is especially the case when this basic theme is challenged and confronted by the biblical truth that God's laws are the ultimate criteria for right and wrong.

The Effects of Personal and Corporate Sin

Whereas the fall of humanity has had a widespread and general effect on human culture and cultural themes, personal sins and corporate sins of a society have a more direct impact on the themes. Personal sins affect each individual's perception and use of the cultural themes. Corporate sins of the society or sinful decisions made by the leadership can shape the content, expression, and dominance of the themes. Corporate sin can occur as a result of group decisions, acts of war, nationally approved or tolerated atrocities (e.g., Nazi Germany and the Jews), alliances with other nations, religious rituals, etc.

Group decisions often lead to alliances, which entail compromises or agreements, which in turn alter existing themes or create new ones.[111] The German theme of *Ordnung* was significantly impacted by the Germans' decision to allow the Nazi party into power through the elections. It was a decision subconsciously driven by the desire to restore order in a country that was plagued by economic and social chaos during the 1920s and early 1930s. On one hand, the Nazi government provided much needed order, stability, and national self-

---

[111] It is important to note that not all alliances are negative. Some alliances will establish or promote the God-given purpose and functions of the themes.

worth, which had been missing. On the other hand, it redefined how order was to be understood and achieved. It was coupled with a number of sinful and destructive compromises. The most notable of these was the officially approved persecution of the Jewish people. The elections officially sanctioned the Nazi ideology and belief that the Jews were the main cause for the economic and social disorder. The theme of *Ordnung* was significantly impacted by this distorted and perverted view.

The Effects of the Sins of the Cultural Gatekeepers

A third way sin impacts and distorts themes is through the sins and actions of the cultural gatekeepers. A cultural gatekeeper like Adolf Hitler had an enormous effect on how the German society understood and lived out their theme of *Ordnung*. Hitler and his corrupted ideology and use of power shaped and redefined this theme. Maintaining order and discipline were of the highest priority to him. Through his leadership and persuasive powers, his understanding of *Ordnung* received a disproportionate emphasis in German society.

The Distortions of Cultural Themes

How are the cultural themes distorted by human sinfulness? Through sin the content of the cultural themes can become twisted and perverted, creating assumptions and premises, which exclude the divine perspective and directives from the society. Some themes may still contain their original content, but become associated with sinful and ungodly expressions. This is often the case when themes become synonymous with ungodly gatekeepers. Likewise, wrongly interpreting them or using them in a sinful way can distort the themes. Themes can become the means by which ungodly and destructive power structures are implemented or maintained in a society.

The distortion can appear in various forms. (1) The themes can become the center of worship. Over time, the content or an expression of the theme becomes absolutized. It becomes the focus of a society's trust leading to its worship. There is a tendency among societies and nations to elevate one's self as absolute and worship its ideals or themes. The gods and objects of worship are representations or embodiments of the culture's ideals and its dominant cultural themes.[112]

George Eldon Ladd states that in the New Testament Jewish life, the law theme had become the focus of their worship. "The fundamental sin of the Jews who have the Law is 'boasting', i.e., perverting the Law so that it becomes the basis of self-confidence that seeks glory before God and relies upon

---

[112] Wink, *Unmasking the Powers*, 95.

itself."[113] From a missiological perspective, the redirecting of worship from the Creator to the created is the most serious and detrimental impact that sin-influenced themes can have on a society.

(2) The distortion creates a disproportionate dominance by the theme in the society. As stated above, some themes can become so dominant that they bring about an unhealthy balance in a society. These themes control all other themes and function as the overriding, single controlling theme. The counter themes no longer function as the needed balance.

(3) The themes can lead a society into unhealthy and destructive alliances, emphases, pursuits, and focuses. Instead of leading the people into a relationship with God and a reliance on his sovereign power and provision, they lead the society to place their confidence and trust in either their own, this-worldly, or supernatural powers. This reliance is upheld through various compromises as well as culturally accepted rituals and traditions.

(4) The themes can become the stepping-stone for ungodly behavior. In some cases the themes can promote actions and behavior disapproved of in Scripture. The behavior is justified and labeled acceptable in the society because it coincides with the theme.

(5) The distorted themes can create various fears and thinking patterns, which act as strongholds that keep the society captive to illogical and destructive beliefs. The Twabrid tribe in the Philippines was driven by a fear of strangers and new ideas. As a result, the gospel messengers and messages were rejected, not based on their message or merits, but based on their theme-induced fear.[114]

(6) The themes become subject to the manipulation and control of Satan and his demonic powers. Sin opens the door for the demonic powers to use the themes for their rebellious purposes. Through their control, the themes become a part of a bigger coordinated effort in hindering the advancement and acceptance of the gospel. The nature of these powers and their control over cultural themes gained through the sins of a society will be the focus of the next chapter.

(7) The most significant result of distorted themes viewed from a missiological perspective is that they create a resistant heart and keep individuals and societies from hearing and understanding the gospel message. They become vehicles by which people are blinded to the ways of God, pursue and worship created idols, and follow human speculation. J. H. Bavinck writes,

---

[113] George Eldon Ladd, *A Theology of the New Testament* (Grand Rapids: William B. Eerdmans, 1974), 445.

[114] Pennoyer, "Dark Dungeons," 250-56.

within the framework of the non-Christian life, customs and practices serve idolatrous tendencies and drive a person away from God. It creates a collective captivity to perceptions, concepts, ideas, and behavior patterns that support and perpetuate a life without the god of the Gospel.[115]

If missions is to be effective, it needs to take cultural themes seriously and deal with the theme strongholds that have become hindrances to the gospel.

Conclusion

Through the influence of human sin, cultural themes can become a significant barrier to the advancement of the gospel. The themes are not corrupted in their essence, but through human sinfulness the original meaning, the appropriate expression, the proper use, and correct understanding of the themes are distorted and the society's viewpoints, ideas, and behavioral patterns twisted which keep a society from properly hearing and understanding the gospel message. To gain entrance into a society, these themes need to be taken seriously and need to be transformed.

The Impact of Cultural Themes on a People Group's Receptivity to the Gospel

Since cultural themes are an integrated part of culture, which shape the thinking and behavioral patterns of a society and its people, they also have a significant bearing on missions. In the last three decades, missiological anthropology has increasingly focused on the relationship of culture's deep-level structures to missions. Missiologists are becoming more and more conscious of the fact that cultural themes and related concepts (e.g., worldview, deep-level structures, the mentality or personality of a people, etc.) play a significant role in how missions is conducted. They are finding that cultural themes are either helpful or hindering vehicles and realizing that unless they properly understand and deal with the themes, their evangelism and contextualization efforts will be limited. This section will look at the positive and negative influences cultural themes have on the mission process.

Cultural Themes as Vehicles of Assistance

Cultural themes impact missions either in a positive or negative way. In their original state, the cultural themes serve as a useful vehicle in three ways.

---

[115] J. H. Bavinck, *An Introduction to the Science of Missions*, translated by David Hugh Freeman (Phillipsburg, NJ: Presbyterian & Reformed Publishing Co., 1979), 179.

(1) Cultural themes are vehicles for understanding the receptor's culture. The study of cultural themes provides the missionary with insights into the society's way of life. It points out what is important, what is of value, and what the correct code of communication and behavior is in the group. Through knowing and adjusting to the themes, the missionary is able to present himself or herself and the gospel in a more relevant and presentable manner.

(2) Cultural themes are vehicles for introducing and communicating the gospel. Cultural themes can function as the gateway to the hearts of the people. They shape the way the gospel is presented and serve as a guide for communicating the gospel. They deal with issues that are important to the society. If the missionary can tap into and relate to the issues and concepts, he or she is more likely to find a responsive hearing for the gospel. Cultural themes help the missionary find and address the real felt-needs of a society.

(3) Cultural themes are vehicles for effective contextualization. Cultural themes provide a plan and path for effective contextualization. Through the themes, the gospel can be naturally integrated into the culture with relatively few unnecessary clashes. The more the gospel is integrated on this root level, the less chance for syncretism or its rejection on the grounds of being culturally foreign or irrelevant. Its impact will be stronger, more thorough, more effective, and more lasting as it impacts the other areas of culture (e.g., politics, social issues, technology, family life, law, etc.).

Cultural Themes as Vehicles of Hindrance

Cultural themes can also create resistance in a society as they hinder and oppose the gospel. This can occur in a number of different ways, some of which include:

(1) Cultural themes directly conflict with the gospel. The content of the themes may stand in direct or indirect conflict with the basic tenets of the gospel. People have integrated and identified with the themes' assumptions and premises to such an extent that any new teaching that challenges their validity is most likely rejected. Furthermore, the themes are in conflict with the gospel when they have become the center of the society's worship. In some cases, the themes establish thinking and behavioral patterns that will make a society suspicious or antagonistic to any new ideas, including the gospel.

(2) Cultural themes function as the basis for power structures and arrangements that conflict with the gospel. The cultural themes are the means by which leaders, power structures, and forces are established and sustained. In many cases, the gospel is considered a threat to existing powers. They resist

the gospel by twisting and using the themes to oppose the gospel in hope of maintaining the existing power arrangements.

(3) Cultural themes may oppose new ideas, like the gospel, which would lead to cultural instability. The cultural themes provide the culture with stability and direction. When the gospel is viewed as an agent of unwanted change, this can produce a sense of insecurity and fear. In this case, people will hold on to and rally around the cultural themes, using them against the gospel in hope of maintaining the security they receive through the themes. Sometimes people resist the gospel not because they think it is false, but because they perceive it as a threat to their culture, especially when the group's solidarity is threatened.

(4) Cultural themes support an object of worship that is in conflict with the gospel. Cultural themes can become a society's focus of worship or maintain the worship of false gods, sacred objects, or a human leader. Through rituals and continuous worship, the society has deepened their allegiance to the theme-related gods and objects of worship. The themes induce and maintain this false worship. Since the central message of the gospel is the worship of Jesus Christ, it will automatically encounter fierce resistance when the society's themes are tied up with the group's gods, leaders, or objects of worship.

Missiological Responses to Hindering Themes

In light of missions, how should one deal with distorted and perverted cultural themes, which are hostile to the gospel and their messengers? There are three basic ways missions has responded.

(1) Cultural themes are ignored, rejected, or in some cases replaced with new themes. Themes that conflict with Scripture are rejected by the missionary and replaced with biblically founded yet often culturally foreign themes. This approach disregards the deep-rooted, integrated nature of culture and its themes. Evangelism and contextualization take place on a surface level and rarely penetrate the heart of the culture. In most cases, the original theme will remain or return through syncretism or complete rejection of the new Christian-based theme.

(2) Cultural themes are uncritically accepted. Out of respect for the receptor's culture, the themes are accepted as they are and never critically evaluated. The gospel is accommodated to fit the culture. It is integrated into the cultural matrix without dealing with the sinful aspects of the themes. This view states that the gospel, once established, will deal with any corruption affecting the themes. In most cases, this position also leads to forms of syncretism.

(3) Cultural themes are critically evaluated and properly transformed to coincide with biblical principles. The themes are evaluated and either accepted,

rejected, or modified based on their conformity to biblical teachings and principles in the area addressed by the themes (e.g., relationships, defining and explaining reality, classifying, setting priorities, etc.). Missions restores and modifies those themes, which are distorted. The goal is to transform the culture and its themes in order to create a favorable setting in which the gospel and the biblical teachings can be established and can flourish as a culturally integrated entity. The evaluation and transformation process begins before the gospel is introduced and continues as the gospel message establishes itself.

Summary

Cultural themes significantly impact missions. The God-given purpose of the themes is to function as vehicles that support the establishment of the gospel. When the themes fall under the influence of sin, they become distorted in their content and their use and can become a hindrance to evangelism rather than help. One of the goals of missions should be to help transform the themes to their intended purpose so that they can serve their redemptive purpose and function. The transformation process should restore and revitalize the themes rather than change or replace them with new ones. In light of this understanding, it is important to know the themes and understand their make-up and level of impact so that they can be properly dealt with and used for the purpose of evangelism and contextualization.

Conclusion

The student has analyzed the cultural theme concept as it relates to the mission process and has made the following observations. (1) The 'cultural theme' model is a useful anthropological model for understanding the deep-level structures of culture and its worldview. Each society is guided by a number of interrelated themes, with some being more dominant and influential than others. (2) Cultural themes significantly shape the outlook and perception of the society and its people. (3) Cultural themes have both a functional as well as a redemptive purpose. (4) Cultural themes can help or hinder the cause of the gospel. (5) Through the presence of sin, the redemptive purpose of cultural themes has been suppressed and distorted. In many cases, the distorted themes become strongholds, which are the driving force behind the people's resistance and opposition to the gospel. (6) Because of the significance of cultural themes in the society as well as their tremendous influence on the thinking patterns of the people, they need to be taken seriously by those evangelizing and contextualizing the gospel.

This chapter has focused on the visible nature of cultural themes. Yet when dealing with them in the context of missions, it is important not only to know the basic nature and function of the cultural themes, but it is also vital to understand the various spiritual forces that influence and make use of the themes. This chapter has focused on the influence of sin. Within this context, it was pointed out that sin opens the door for the influence of demonic powers. The next chapter will focus on how these powers and forces effect and use cultural themes in order to create hostility and resistance to the gospel. In light of Scripture and current interpretation, it will analyze the relationship between the demonic powers, cultural themes, and missions.

Chapter III
The Relationship of Demonic Powers to Cultural Themes

Introduction

The previous chapter shows that cultural themes shape the matrix of a society and significantly impact evangelism and missions. These themes either function as a natural pathway for introducing and establishing the gospel in a society or become the source of resistance and opposition to the gospel when distorted through individual and corporate sin. The distorted themes keep a society spiritually blinded to the message of the gospel and enslave them to a pattern of thinking and behaving that is in conflict with the truth of the gospel. It is necessary to determine who is responsible for the themes' distortion and to see if sin is the lone corporate in distorting the themes or if there are other forces at work.

Scripture clearly states that the demonic powers keep individuals and people groups from knowing and accepting the gospel (2 Cor. 4:4; Acts 26:18; Eph. 2:1-3). Eph. 6:12 states that "our struggle is not against flesh and blood, but against the rulers, against the powers, against the world forces of this darkness, against the spiritual forces of wickedness in the heavenly places." Who are these demonic powers, and what role do they play in distorting cultural themes?

The study suggests that demonic powers influence and distort structures and cultural themes in order to create demonic strongholds that function as barriers against the gospel. This chapter will analyze the relationship between the demonic powers and cultural themes (powers / theme relationship), as well as analyze and evaluate the current views within the Spiritual Warfare Movement on this issue. A working model of the powers/theme relationship will be presented at the end of the chapter. This model will serve as the basis for chapters 4 and 5.

Since there are many angles to this issue, certain limitations will be made in order to keep the study focused. (1) The student will analyze the demonic from a missiological/theological perspective. The powers/theme relationship will be examined in light of its missiological significance. (2) He will focus on issues and trends related to strategic-level spiritual warfare, which deals with the relationship of the demonic powers to structural and geopolitical entities.[116] It is beyond the scope of this study to deal either with ground level or

---

[116] There are three levels of Spiritual Warfare. (1) *Ground-level Spiritual Warfare* deals with the relationship between the demonic and the individual. (2) *Occult-level*

occult-level spiritual warfare. Issues related to these areas of study will be examined as they relate to the powers/theme relationship.

An Analysis of the Powers / Theme Relationship

The following is an analysis of the relationship between the demonic powers and cultural themes in Scripture and in current interpretation.[117] It will focus on those aspects that shed light on the powers/theme relationship.

Definition of Terms

Before looking more closely at the powers / theme relationship, it is necessary to define the terms 'demonic' and 'demonic powers'.

Definition of 'Demonic'

The title of the dissertation suggests that the distortion of cultural themes is demonic. What does this term imply? The term is used as a category and symbol for evil. It implies that something or someone is either inherently evil or has been overtaken by evil.[118] The demonic distortions indicate that the cultural themes have become evil, which means that they are in conflict with the gospel and function as barriers to the cause of Christ.

'Demonic' denotes the presence or influence of demons or spiritual entities who are in part responsible for the presence of evil. The demonic distortion of cultural themes implies that the themes are either influenced by the demons or

---

Spiritual Warfare deals with the demonic as it relates to witchcraft, Satanism, the New Age Movement, spiritism, and other similar demonic manifestations. (3) *Strategic-level Spiritual Warfare* deals with the demonic powers as they relate to geopolitical territories, social networks, and social and cultural structures. The last level is also referred to as the 'cosmic-level' or 'higher-level' warfare. The focus of most strategic-level spiritual warfare literature has been on 'territorial spirits' who are associated with geopolitical territories, such as communities, cities, and nations. Little has been written about the demonic influences on cultural networks and their structures. The two leading proponents of the strategic-level spiritual warfare position are Wagner and Wink. Kraft and White, *Behind Enemy Lines*, 13.

[117] This presentation is based on P. T. O'Brien's analysis of demonic powers in the article "Principalities and Powers: Opponents of the Church" in *Biblical Interpretation and the Church: Text and Context*, ed. D. A. Carson (Grand Rapids: Baker Books, 1984).

[118] The concept of evil will not be further developed in this study. In this context, evil will be defined as anything that is in rebellion to God or which hinders the cause of Christ.

are under their control. Both the origin and historical usage of the term suggest this understanding. The terms 'demon' and 'demonic' are derived from the Greek term *daimoni,* which originally referred to one of the lesser gods or spirits that attended, indwelt, or ministered to humans and controlled their fate.[119] Initially, the term referred to both benevolent as well as malevolent beings. Under the influence of scripture, it took on a negative connotation and exclusively referred to harmful and destructive beings.

Since the 19th century, as a result of the shift from a supernatural to a materialistic, scientific worldview, many theologians have abandoned the ontological designation of the term and have opted for an exclusive phenomenological understanding. The association of the demonic with a personal spiritual being has been dismissed as naive and mythological.[120] In the second half of the twentieth century, there has been a tendency among theologians, missiologists, and Christian ministers to reevaluate their position on the demonic and return to the original ontological understanding of the term.

This study will incorporate both aspects of the term. Thus in this study, 'demonic' is defined as opposition and rebellion to God and the cause of Christ, which has been brought about by evil spiritual entities which themselves are in rebellion to God.

Definition of "Demonic Powers"

Demonic powers is the collective term used for all independent, personal spiritual entities who are in rebellion to God, oppose his redemptive purposes, and who exert power, control and influence over individuals, social networks, structures, and territories. This designation is preferred over the term 'demon', which is the designation for the individual spiritual being. It is beyond the scope of the study to deal with the individual nature or characteristics of the various demons, nor will it deal with the hierarchical breakdown or the interrelationship of the demonic forces. The study will primarily deal with the demonic powers as a collective entity.

---

[119] For a detailed discussion of the origin and development of the term 'demonic' see Mircea Eliade, ed., *The Encyclopedia of Religion* (New York: Macmillan Pub., 1987), s.v. "Demons," by J. Bruce Long; Karel van der Toorn, Bob Becking, Pieter W. van der Horst, eds., *Dictionary of Deities and Demons in the Bible* (New York: E. J. Brill, 1995), s.v. "Demon," by G. J. Riley.

[120] Wink sums up this sentiment: "We moderns cannot bring ourselves by any feat of will or imagination to believe in the real existence of these mythological entities that traditionally have been lumped under the general category 'principalities and powers'." Wink, *Naming the Powers*, 4.

The term 'demonic powers' points out two characteristics of spiritual beings. (1) They are beings of power. They have a God-given power and authority to influence, rule over and control individuals, social networks and their structures, and geopolitical territories. The spiritual beings originally received the power to serve God and assist humanity. Through their rebellion, the power has become distorted and perverted. Through human sin, the demonic powers reassert this once legitimate power over individuals and people groups, keeping them from worshipping God. Even though the concept of 'power' is an important issue in the study of the demonic powers, it is beyond the scope of this study to deal with the 'power' concept in any detail. (2) The beings are demonic. They are spiritual beings who are inherently evil and in rebellion against God. These two characteristics play a central role in the study's understanding of the demonic powers.

There are various viewpoints as to the exact nature and function of the powers. These views will be discussed in detail later in the chapter. At this point, note that this study assumes that the demonic powers are independent, personal, and spiritual beings. It will show that this position coincides with the biblical understanding of the demonic powers.

A Biblical Analysis of the Power / Theme Relationship

The demonic powers play a significant role in Scripture.[121] Their presence is mentioned or referred to in most of the books of the Bible. Scripture does not present an independent systematized demonology, but always addresses the powers within the context of the human-divine relationship. Dealing with the powers is an important part of God's redemptive plan for humanity.

The Old and New Testament approach and view the powers differently. References to the demonic powers are relatively rare in the Old Testament, whereas in the New Testament, the powers are more prevalent. Jesus' conflict with Satan and the powers is a leading motif in both the Gospels and the Epistles. In the Old Testament, the demonic powers are related to the gods of the nations and are depicted as forces that lead people away from the true worship of God. In the New Testament, the powers represent those forces that oppose

---

[121] For further studies on the demonic powers in Scripture, see Sydney H. T. Page, *Powers of Evil: A Biblical Study of Satan and Demons* (Grand Rapids: Baker Books, 1995), 179. Thomas N. Finger and Willard M. Swartley, "Deliverance and Bondage: Biblical and Theological Perspectives," in *Essays on Spiritual Bondage and Deliverance*, Occasional Papers no. 11, ed. Willard M. Swartley (Elkhart, IN: Institute of Mennonite Studies, 1988), 130-38; and Edward F. Murphy, *The Handbook for Spiritual Warfare* (Nashville: Thomas Nelson Pub., 1992).

the coming of God's kingdom and keep people from a relationship with Jesus Christ.

The Gospels and the Epistles also differ in their approach. The Gospels deal with the demonic powers as they relate to individuals. The central message of Christ's proclamation is God's victory over the kingdom of darkness. Both Jesus and his disciples took a pragmatic approach in demonstrating this message and dealing with the demonic. Casting out demons and enabling his disciples to do the same characterized Jesus' ministry. His method of dealing with the demonic differed substantially from the popular methods of that day. He took authority over the demonic world and did not rely on higher authorities or magical incantations. In his death and resurrection, he defeated and disarmed the demonic powers.

In contrast to the Gospels, the Epistles deal with the demonic powers as a collective entity and emphasize the general influence and position of the powers. The Epistles either address the powers in the context of Christ's victory over the powers (e.g., Col. 2:10), in the context of warning the believers of their threat and danger (e.g., Eph. 6:10), or in the context of showing the nature of their influence over nonbelievers (e.g., 2 Cor. 4:4). The most extensive treatments of the powers are found in Ephesians and Colossians, as well as Revelation.

A Survey of Biblical Teaching on the Demonic Powers

The Origin of the Demonic Powers

Little has been written about the powers before the fall. All that Scripture clearly affirms is that the powers are part of God's creation and under his rule (Col. 1:16; Rom. 8:38-39). There are three primary theories as to the origin of the evil powers. (1) They are disembodied spirits of a pre-Adamic race, destroyed by God. (2) They are the "Nephilim" of Gen. 6:1-4, the disembodied spirits created by the mating of angels with humans. (3) They are angels who fell with Lucifer.[122] It is most likely that some, if not all of the powers, were originally angels. Scripture is clear that certain angels were originally placed over nations and people groups to assist and watch over them (Deut. 31:8).

The powers were created as spiritual beings and currently function as such (Eph. 6:11-12). Stott makes the point that the three references to principalities and powers in Ephesians also contain a reference 'in the heavenly places',

---

[122] Thomas B. White, *The Believer's Guide to Spiritual Warfare* (Ann Arbor, MI: Servant Pub., 1990), 32.

indicating that the powers are spiritual beings who are part of the unseen spiritual world.[123]

The Fall of the Demonic Powers

The awareness that there were fallen spiritual beings developed gradually in Scripture. In the early writings of the Old Testament, these beings were understood, as messengers of God who exercised his will. The clear separation between evil and good spirits, the concept of Satan as God's chief adversary, and the understanding that there are evil, rebellious powers working under Satan's command who are in opposition to God, did not emerge until the postexilic writings.[124] D. S. Russell describes the development of biblical understanding as follows: "There gradually grew up, no doubt under the influence of foreign thought, the notion that the angels to whom God had given authority over the nations and over the physical universe itself, had outstripped their rightful authority and had taken the power into their own hands."[125]

There are various passages in the Old and New Testament that either refer to or imply that the powers have fallen. Some interpret Ezek. 28:12-19 and Isa. 14:12-15 as references to Satan's fall.[126] Gen. 6:1-4, Psalm 82, and other passages state that the powers have committed sins. Isa. 24:21-22 points out that

---

[123] John R. W. Stott, "Principalities and Powers," in *Spiritual Warfare*, ed. John Wimber (Anaheim, CA: Mercy Pub., 1988), 155.

[124] This paradigm shift occurred during the Exilic Period when Jewish people came into contact with Zoroastrianism and other Persian dualistic religions. Scholars differ as to the exact nature of their influence on the development of the demonology in Jewish thought. It is apparent that there was much sharing and borrowing that took place between cultures during this time. There was a general awareness and preoccupation with the presence of evil in the ancient world, which precipitated the development of a more adequate cosmology among cultures of that time. Dualism emerged and significantly shaped most of the ancient religions. In contrast to the other religions, the demonology in Scripture developed within the framework of Jewish monotheism. It borrowed concepts from the dualistic thought, but was not determined by it. In neither the Old Testament nor the New Testament does the battle between good and evil ever become an absolute dualism. Scripture and Jewish demonology continued to stress God's sovereignty over the powers. For discussion on this issue, see J. B. Russell, *The Prince of Darkness* (Ithaca, NY: Cornell University Press, 1988), 17-27, 39-42, 48-51.

[125] D. S. Russell, *The Method of Jewish Apocalyptic* (Philadelphia: Westminster Press, 1964), 237.

[126] Merrill F. Unger, *Biblical Demonology* (Grand Rapids: Kregel Pub., 1994), 15. Sydney Page argues against this interpretation. Based on the historical and grammatical context, he believes these passages refer to human rulers. Page, 37-42.

the powers will be punished for their disobedience. Dan. 10:13, 20-21 shows that the princes of Persia and Greece stood in rebellion to God. In the New Testament, the fall is implied in Jude 6 and 2 Pet. 2:4. Col. 2:14-15 and Eph. 6:12 imply that the powers are rebellious and exert their God-given power in an independent way. Even though there are plenty of speculations, scripture is silent about the reasons for the fall.

Christ's Defeat of the Demonic Powers

The demonic powers have been defeated and disarmed by Jesus Christ on the cross (Col. 2:14-15). This triumph and Christ's lordship (Eph. 1:20-23) over the powers are major themes in the New Testament and the primary context for understanding and dealing with the powers. The reason for Christ's coming was to destroy the work of the Devil (1 John 3:8). Christ has authority over Satan and his demons and was himself victorious over Satan's attacks (Matt. 4:1-11; Matt. 16:21-23). Through the Spirit of God, Jesus had power to cast out the evil spirits (Matt. 12:38). He bound the powers and released men and women from Satan's captivity (Matt. 12:26), delegated the authority to exorcise the powers to his disciples (Mark 3:14-15; Matt. 10:1; Luke 9:1f), and called his followers to release men and women from Satan's domain (Acts 26:18).

The victory over the demonic took place in the death and resurrection of Christ (Col. 1:20, 2:14-15; Heb. 2:14-15). He disarmed the powers and has been placed over them (Eph. 1:20-23; Col. 2:15; Rom. 8:38-39). In Christ, people share in the victory and authority over the powers (Col. 2:20). Because of their participation in Christ's death and resurrection, Christians are called to resist and stand firm against the powers (Eph. 6:10-18).

Glasser summarizes the impact of Christ's victory as follows:

> Their [demonic powers] ancient grip on people has been broken. What remains is merely the capacity for colossal deception ... Although they will continue to divert people from all preoccupation with God himself, their activity is now devoid of substantial power. All is bluff and illusion. It is as though by the cross Christ deliberately disconnected all the linkages within cultures by which the powers previously held people in bondage.[127]

---

[127] Arthur F. Glasser, "Kingdom and Mission," unpublished manuscript, School of World Missions, Fuller Theological Seminary, 1989, 311.

Continued Hostility

In spite of Christ's victory over the powers and their disarmament, they continue to operate in this current age. The victory has yet to be fully implemented. Currently Satan and his powers are still active, influencing, and controlling the world (Eph. 2:1-3; John 12:31). They continue to enslave the unbelievers and harass the Christians (Eph. 2:1-3; 2 Cor. 4:4; 1 Pet. 5:8). However, their power is devoid of substantial power. They rule and operate through the power of deception and distortion (Rev. 12:9). Even though God has allowed Satan and his forces to remain active in the time leading up to Christ's second coming, he has provided the means and authority to resist and overcome the demonic powers (Eph. 6:10-18; 1 John 4:4; 1 Cor. 10:3-5) and has provided assurance that "nothing can separate us from the wonderful love of God" (Rom. 8:38-39).

The Nature of the Demonic Powers' Influence

The powers impact the world at every level. The demonic powers can demonize both believers and unbelievers (Matt. 9:32-33; Matt. 16:13-20; Acts 5:3),[128] work through events and circumstances (Job 1 and 2; Rev. 2:10; 1 Thess. 2:18), and illnesses (Matt. 9:32; 12:22; Luke 9:42). The demonic powers are associated with false teachings, ideologies, and heresy (2 Cor. 11:13-15, 2 Cor. 10:3-5; 1 Tim. 4:1). In the Old Testament, they are associated with gods of the nations (Deut. 32:17; Ps. 96:5; Ps. 106:37).[129] Col. 2:20 relates the demonic powers to the "elemental spirits of the world." Many of the New Testament terms for the powers (e.g., principalities, dominions, thrones, princes and rulers, lords) imply that they are associated with individuals and structures of authority and power. These include influential people, governments and their rulers, as well as social, political, economic and religious structures. The demonic powers use these various events, structures, and individuals to establish dominions and strongholds, which keep people captive and blinded from the gospel (Acts 26:18; 2 Cor. 4:4; 1 Cor. 10:3-5). Scripture shows that sin opens the door for demonic activity (Acts 5:1-3; 1 Cor. 5:4-5; 2 Cor. 2:10-11; 1 Tim. 3:6-7).

---

[128] The issue of 'Demonization versus Demon Possession' and the question, "Can Christians be demon possessed?" is beyond the scope of the study. For discussion on these issues, see Arnold, *3 Crucial Questions*, 73-141; and C. Fred Dickason, *Demon Possession and the Christian*, rev. ed. (Chicago: Moody Press, 1987).

[129] The Hebrew term *sedim*, which is used in reference to the gods in the listed verses, is translated by the LXX with the Greek word *daimonion*. The rabbinical tradition as well as the early church fathers associated the gods of the nations with the demonic powers. Page, 65-68; Finger and Swartley, 13.

The Christian Response to the Powers

Scripture continuously warns the Christian about the demonic threat (1 Pet. 5:8; Eph. 4:27). Yet, Christians are to live in Christ's victory, give thanks (Col. 1:12-14), and express confidence and boldness in the face of this threat (1 John 2:13; 4:4; 5:4, 18). Christians are to resist (James 4:7), stand firm against (Eph. 6:10), overcome (1 John 5:40; Rev. 12:11), and exorcise (Mark 3:15) the demonic powers. Eph. 6:10-18 provides the clearest exposition of the Christians' stance. They are to resist with truth (v. 14), righteousness (v. 14), faith (v. 15), salvation (v. 17), prayer [intercession] (v. 18), by taking up the word of God (v. 17), sharing the gospel (v. 15), and being watchful (v. 18; 1 Pet. 5:18). It is important to note that there is no direct mandate in Scripture to engage directly or cast out "territorial spirits."

There are two basic approaches to dealing with the demonic based on this passage. The conservative approach states that Christians are to resist and take a defensive stance against the powers. The more aggressive approach believes Christians are not only to resist but also aggressively confront the powers, overcome them, and cast them out in order to advance the kingdom. This view is based on Jesus' example and his commission to his disciples.

Rev. 12:1 lists three aspects of how Christians will overcome the evil one: (1) "by the blood of the lamb", (b) "by the word of their testimony", and (c) "they did not love their lives so much to shrink from death." It is important to note that in most listings concerning the Christian's response there is no mention of seeking out or directly addressing the demonic powers. In the Old Testament, dealing with the demonic powers occurs by being faithful to God and destroying the gods of false worship (Exod. 23:24; Deut. 12:29).

The Powers' Influence on Missions and Evangelism

The demonic powers still maintain a hold on unbelievers, relentlessly attack the church, and thwart the advancement of God's kingdom among the nations. They are blocking the mind, emotion, and will of the people through directly influencing individuals, distorting human structures, and creating personal and structural strongholds. Unbelievers are called children of Satan (Eph. 2:2), they are part of Satan's kingdom (Col. 1:12-14), bound by Satan (Acts 26:18), blinded by the god of this age (2 Cor. 4:4), are part of a world system controlled by Satan (1 John 5:19) and are living in darkness and captivity (Eph. 2:1-3, 4:17-18, 5:8). Even though the powers still exert their influence over people, they cannot ultimately hinder the advancement of the gospel.

Matt. 12:25-26 identifies Satan and his powers as strongmen who hold people captive, but who now have been bound by Christ. The disciples are called to plunder the strongman's possession and help release the captives. This verse implies that the demonic strongman is a significant part of the evangelism process.[130] Christ has come to release the captives, restore sight to the blind, and set people free (Isa. 42:6; Matt. 4:16; Luke 1:78-79; 1 Pet. 2:9). Christians are to join with the Holy Spirit in helping people out of their captivity and opening their eyes to the gospel (Acts 26:18). Through the church, the powers are confronted with God's redemptive purpose for mankind (Eph. 3:10). The church is to bear witness and demonstrate God's redemptive purpose. Jesus Christ has delegated his authority to his disciples in order to deal with the powers (Luke 10:1, 17-19). Casting out demons is part of the gospel proclamation (Mark 3:1; Matt. 10:7-8). Other missionary tools mentioned in Scripture, which deal with the demonic powers include prayer, the gospel, and the word of God (Eph. 6:10-18). Rom. 12:14-21 states that evil is to be overcome not by evil but by love and doing good.

The Demonic Powers' Final Defeat

The current activity of the powers will come to an end when Christ returns. He will abolish all rule and authority (1 Cor. 15:24-28). Satan and the powers will be judged, punished, and cast into the lake of fire (Rev. 20:10).

An Evaluation of the Biblical Teaching on the Demonic Powers' Relationship to Structures and Cultural Themes

The Demonic in the Context of the Ancients' View of Reality

The prevailing ancient worldview and the first-century Jewish demonology shaped Scripture's approach to the demonic powers. Four basic assumptions prevailed in antiquity. (1) They believed in a supernatural dimension with spiritual beings. (2) They assumed an active interaction between the forces of the invisible and visible world. Michael Green points out that there was "such a correspondence between the world of sense and time and the invisible world that the two were, to the ancients, almost a single entity."[131] (3) To the ancients, all aspects of life were subject to the influence and control of the spir-

---

[130] There is a debate whether the verse refers to Jesus as the binder or is to be seen as a mandate for the Christians. Wagner and other Third Wave proponents view this passage as a commissioning passage, which gives the believers a mandate and the authority to bind and cast out the demonic powers directly. They associate the concept of binding with the terms overcoming and casting out. This is a key passage for the Third Wave-oriented approach to strategic-level spiritual warfare. For Wagner's full explanation of his position, see C. Peter Wagner, "Spiritual Warfare", in *Engaging the Enemy*, ed. C. Peter Wagner (Ventura, CA: Regal Books, 1991), 14-15.

[131] Michael Green, *Exposing the Prince of Darkness* (Ann Arbor, MI: Servant Books, 1981), 81.

itual forces.¹³² (4) The conflict between good and evil was viewed in dualistic terms.¹³³

Scripture affirmed the basic premises of the first three worldview assumptions, but rejected its dualistic view of reality. Even though the battle between good and evil is a central issue in both the antiquities' and Scripture's view of reality, Scripture's view differed in its understanding of the conflict. Good and evil were never portrayed as two equal forces. The biblical writers always viewed reality and the powers' influence and control in the context of God's sovereignty. The goal of the conflict differed as well. The objective of the battle was not to defeat one's foes or to gain power over them, but to bring about God's peace and to lead God's creation into right relationship with him. The means of battle was not power, but the way of the cross.¹³⁴

A second significant influence was the popular first-century Jewish demonology. Many references and practices in the New Testament dealing with the demonic powers can only be understood within the context of popular understanding of the demonic world. The interest in the spiritual reality and the belief in the demonic powers flourished during the intertestamental period. Arnold states that "this preoccupation with the spirit world can be traced in virtually all facets of its literature – the Old Testament, Apocryphal writings (especially Tobit), the Qumran literature, the pseudepigraphal testamentary literature and particularly in the Jewish apocalyptic writings."¹³⁵ They speculated about the nature of the beings, their names, their hierarchy, as well as the nature of the demonic influence over nations and social structures.¹³⁶ Most of the apocryphal writings make frequent reference to the demonic powers.¹³⁷

---

[132] The belief prevailed that spiritual beings occupied the intermediary regions between the heavens and earth and either assisted or hindered the communication between humans and the gods. These powers not only impacted individuals, but were also seen as the forces behind political, social, cultural, economic, and religious structures and institutions, as well as those forces influencing and controlling the rulers and leaders.

[133] For further study of the ancient worldviews as they relate to the study of the demonic powers in Scripture, see Russell, *Prince of Darkness*, 7-55; and Arnold, *Powers of Darkness*, 19-74.

[134] Hiebert, "Spiritual Warfare," chap. in *Anthropological Reflections on Missiological Issues* (Grand Rapids: Baker Books, 1994), 209-13.

[135] Arnold, *Powers of Darkness*, 64.

[136] In the War Scrolls (1QM), one of the Dead Sea Scrolls, Satan and the evil forces are associated with the Romans (1 QM 13:4-5). Arnold states: "The scroll sees the battle taking place on two dimensions, with men fighting men and angels fighting angels. There is, however, a crossover in which the good angels are portrayed as help-

Scripture affirmed the basic Jewish demonology, but did not deal with the demonic world in the same manner or with the same frequency. The biblical writers remained focused on the human-divine relationship and did not make the demonic powers a central issue, nor were they interested in establishing a demonology. They did not engage in the lofty speculations, exaggerations, magical practices, or superstitions common in those days.

The writers consistently dealt with the people's fears and concerns about the spiritual forces that controlled their lives. They addressed the powers in the context of God's sovereignty, Christ's lordship over the powers, and as part of God's plan of redemption.[138] Scripture provided a new way to deal with and overcome the forces of darkness, which held the people captive.

The Demonic within the Context of God's Sovereignty and Man's Responsibility

The biblical view of the demonic is consistent with the doctrine of God's sovereignty and the doctrine of man's moral agency. God's sovereignty is maintained throughout Scripture. The powers are created beings and even in their fallenness are subject to God's power. This is in contrast to the dualism propagated by most ancient religions.[139]

Scripture also maintains human responsibility for his or her choices. In contrast to the popular view in antiquity in which humans were helpless victims of demonic activity, Scripture guards the dignity of human choice. Ladd observes:

> The doctrine of Satan and demons has several distinct theological implications. Evil is not imposed upon people directly by God, nor is evil blind chance or capricious fate. Evil has its roots in personality. Yet evil

---

ing God's people and Satan's hosts as helping the Roman soldiers." Ibid., 65.

[137] For further study on first-century Jewish demonology, see D. S. Russell, *Jewish Apocalyptic*, 235-62; and W. O. E. Oesterley, "Angelology and Demonology in Early Judaism," in *A Companion to the Bible*, ed. T. W. Manson (Edinburgh: T & T Clark, 1939), 332-47.

[138] Unger, 25; Ladd, 48; and Adrio König, *The Eclipse of Christ in Eschatology* (Grand Rapids: William Eerdmans Pub., 1989), 124.

[139] Ladd states: "Neither in Judaism nor in the New Testament does this antithetical kingdom of evil opposing the Kingdom of God become an absolute dualism. The fallen angels are helpless before the power of God and his angels. In the New Testament, all such spiritual powers are creatures of God and therefore subject to his power. In the apocalyptic literature, they will meet their doom in the day of judgment." Ladd, 48. Also see Unger, 25f; and Page, 82.

is greater than human beings. It can be resisted by human will, although the human will can yield to it.[140]

Scripture affirms the triad of evil composed of the flesh, the world, and Satan (demonic powers). The powers orchestrate temptation, deception, and accusations by exerting their influence and control wherever permitted. Even though humans are subject to these forces, they are ultimately responsible for their sins and the resulting evil. Through sin the powers are able to exert their influence and control over individuals and structures.[141] Even though evil is associated with the demonic realm, human responsibility for the presence of evil is always maintained and emphasized in both the Old and the New Testament.

Terminology in Referring to the Demonic Powers

Scripture uses a rich vocabulary in referring to the demonic powers, which provide information about their function, character, nature, and realm of operation. The Old Testament uses terms such as 'sons of God' (Gen. 6:1-4); 'gods' (Psalm 82; Deut. 32:17; Ps. 106:37; Ps. 96:4-5); 'powers in the heavens' (Isa. 24:21-22); 'princes' (Dan. 10:13, 20-21, 12:1); and 'evil spirits' (e.g., 1 Kings 22:19-23 and 2 Chron. 18:18-22) to refer to demonic beings.[142]

Significant New Testament terms include 'principalities' (*archai*), 'powers' (*exousiai, dynameis*), 'dominions' (*kyriotetes*), 'thrones' (*thronoi*), 'names' (*onoma*), 'angels' (*angeloi*), 'princes and rulers' (*archontes*), 'lords' (*kyrioi*), 'gods' (*theoi*), 'demons' (*daimonia*), 'spirits' (*pneumata*), 'the basic principles of the world' (*ta stoicheia tou kosmou*), 'angels of nations', 'unclean spirits', 'spirit of wickedness', 'world forces of darkness', and 'rulers of this age'.[143] Most of these terms appear in the Pauline letters and are found as part of a listing of terms. The most notable passages referring to the powers in the New

---

[140] Ladd, 48.

[141] Unger, 27.

[142] Page gives a detailed discussion about the Old Testament usage of these terms. Even though there are some who question the association of these terms to spiritual beings, Page successfully shows that they refer to demonic beings. Page, 43-82. There are many other references and terms in the Old Testament which may possibly refer to demonic powers. However, most are questionable references. In most cases, they either lack sufficient evidence or are based on comparative speculation. See Page 83-86.

[143] For a more extended list of New Testament terms, see Heinrich Schlier, *Principalities and Powers in the New Testament* (London: Burns & Oates, 1961), 11f. For a detailed discussion on the meaning of the Old Testament and New Testament terms, see van der Toorn, Becking, and van der Horst, *Dictionary of Deities*.

Testament include Rom. 8:38-39; 1 Cor. 15:24-27; Eph. 1:18-21; Eph. 3:10; Eph. 6:12; Col. 1:15-20; Col. 2:10, 15.

The terms can refer to both evil and good spirits. In some passages the terms refer exclusively to the demonic powers (Eph. 2:1-3, 6:12; Col. 1:15-20). Other passages are unclear if the terms refer exclusively to rebellious spirits or include all spiritual beings (Rom. 8:38-39; Eph. 3:10). In some, it is clear that the passages refer to both (Eph. 1:21; Col. 2:15).[144]

Terms referring to Satan include 'Devil', 'Beelzebub', 'Beliar', 'serpent', 'the lion', 'the evil one', 'the liar', 'the accuser', 'the destroyer', 'the adversary', 'the enemy', 'prince of demons', 'prince of this world', 'prince of the power of the air', etc. In scripture the distinction between Satan and demons is often blurred. Page notes: "For the most part, the Epistles and Revelation attribute the same functions to evil spirits that they attribute to the devil himself."[145]

The biblical terms for the demonic powers are not proper names, but terms, which reveal the purpose, nature, and function of the powers. The various terms show that they function as beings of power who rule over and influence people, dominions, and principalities. They have become the objects of people's worship. They are associated with various sins. They lie, deceive, tempt, accuse, and seek to destroy humans and God's other creations. They are characterized as unclean, wicked, world forces, and fallen. They are by nature powers, God's creation, and spiritual beings. They operate in the world, in this age, and are situated in the heavenlies.

The Demonic Powers As Independent, Personal, Spiritual Beings

The powers are spiritual beings. They reside and operate in the heavenlies. Green points out that

---

[144] Recently Wesley Carr has suggested that these references to the powers refer to entities that stood in a positive relationship to God. With the exception of Eph. 6:12, which he does not view as being part of the original Pauline text, all references to the powers are to non-hostile beings. Carr tried to show that the idea that evil forces afflict humans was not part of the early Christian understanding of the gospel. Wesley Carr, *Angels and Principalities* (Cambridge, Cambridge University, 1981). This position stands in stark contrast to most scholarly interpretations of these passages. In O'Brien's critique of Carr, he questions Carr's understanding of the first-century Jewish worldview, his basic theological presuppositions, and his handling of Eph. 6:12. O'Brien, 125-29. It is beyond the scope of this study to deal with the good powers or to analyze their relationship with the demonic powers.

[145] Page, 260.

> the main thrust of the New Testament teaching is to see these powers as spiritual entities in "the heavenlies" i.e., the spiritual world ... [It] makes it almost impossible to believe that earthly forces are in view. This does not for one moment mean that the principalities and powers may not infest government, public opinion and the like. It simply avoids the confusion of identifying them.[146]

They are independent powers. They are associated with and relate to individuals, structures, governments, ideologies, institutions, and forces of nature, yet they are not equated or identified with any of these in Scripture. Scripture clearly differentiates between the demonic powers and the object of their interest and possession (Mark 5:1-13).

Scripture assumes the personal nature of the demonic powers, but remains relatively silent as to its meaning. Hans Rohrbach believes that the powers are perceived as personal because they manifest themselves as personal beings. They are more than just the negation of good.[147]

Michael Green suggests that the powers are personal in their essence. They are personal in the same sense as humans are personal in that they are a distinct being with an organizing spiritual intellect, created by God, who can speak and be spoken to and who are capable of following or rebelling against God's will. However, they are different in that they stand in a different relationship to God as human beings. They have not become incarnate nor do they share in the human condition.[148]

Scripture depicts the demonic powers as spiritual beings who can influence and possess humans and who are associated, but not equated with earthly objects, structures, ideologies, institutions, social networks, and geopolitical areas. They are intellectual beings who manifest themselves in a personal manner.

---

[146] Green, 85.

[147] Rohrbach states: "In gleicher Weise liegt auch über der Personhaftigkeit des Bösen, des Teufels, ein Geheimnis, das die Bibel nicht preisgibt. Auch er ist Geist, Macht und Person und wirkt deshalb personhaft auf den Menschen, weil er sich in konkreten Anläufen so manifestiert. In der Manifestation liegt das Personhafte." Hans Rohrbach, *Unsicthbare Mächte und die Macht Jesus* (Wuppertal, R. Brockhaus Verlag, 1985), 33.

[148] Green, 30.

A Functional Relationship between the Earthly Structures and Spiritual Powers

Even though Scripture's primary focus is the natural realm, it supplies sufficient evidence that there is a cause and effect relationship between the natural and supernatural realms. Dan. 10:1-21 provides the most in-depth insight into the spiritual battle being fought in the heavenlies and its effect on the natural realm. The text shows that events in the heavenlies affect the natural. Page points out that "the portrayal of the princes of the nations in Daniel reveals that the unfolding of human history is not determined solely by the decisions made by human beings, for there is an unseen dimension of reality that must also be taken into account."[149] The message intended for Daniel was delayed because of the spiritual battle. At the same time, the text implies that prayer affects events in the spiritual world.[150]

This interrelationship between the two dimensions is also evident in the biblical terminology used for the powers. Most of the terms are used for the demonic powers as well as the natural power structures. In an attempt to find the proper relationship between the demonic powers and structures, the twofold usage has been interpreted in two different ways.

The Both / And Position

The terms are understood as interchangeable, referring to *both* the natural structures *and* the spiritual powers in its various uses. R. J. Sider notes: "There is growing agreement that when St. Paul speaks of the principalities and powers ...he refers both to the socio-political structures of human society and to unseen spiritual forces that undergird, lie behind and in some mysterious way help shape human socio-political structures."[151]

Wink, in his book *Naming the Powers*, has tried to establish an interpretive framework for this position.[152] He contends, "the language of power in the New Testament is imprecise, liquid, interchangeable, and unsystematic" as well as "far too rich and complex to reduce either to the human structures and

---

[149] Page, 65.

[150] For a discussion of the various interpretations of Daniel 10, see Page, 63-65 and Robert J. Priest, Thomas Campbell, and Bradford A. Mullen, "Missiological Syncretism: The New Animistic Paradigm," in *Spiritual Power and Missions: Raising the Issues*, ed. Edward Rommen (Pasadena, CA: William Carey Library, 1995), 70-76.

[151] Ron J. Sider, "Christ and Power," *International Review of Missions* 69 (January 1980): 17.

[152] Wink, *Naming the Powers*, 15.

institutions of the liberation theologians or to the spiritual beings of traditional theology."[153] He therefore concludes "unless the context further specifies (and some do), we are to take the terms for power in their most comprehensive sense, understanding them to mean both heavenly and earthly, divine and human, good and evil powers."[154] Cullman presents a similar both/and understanding of the language.[155] Based on the interchangeable terminology, the both/and position equates and identifies the powers with the structures.

The Either/Or Position

A clear ontological distinction is made between the demonic powers and human structures. The various terms *either* refers to human structures *or* spiritual beings, but not both. Green and Arnold reject the notion that the terms are "imprecise, interchangeable and unsystematic" and point out that the use of the power terminology in Scripture as well as in other contemporary texts, with few exceptions, clearly indicate an either/or distinction.[156] As a result, the "either/or" position maintains an ontological separation between the powers and earthly entities. The definition of the relationship between the powers and the earthly structures is based on the nature of their interaction, rather than a common terminology.

Even though there is a clear distinction in the usage of the terms, the common functional language suggests an interrelationship based on the phenomena, function, and character expressed in the terms. The language indicates that both the earthly structures and the powers rule, have authority, and exert power over people and areas. It is unlikely that either Paul or the other biblical writers intended to equate the spiritual powers and the natural structures based on the common terminology. It can be assumed, however, that they perceived

---

[153] Ibid., 9, 15.

[154] Ibid., 39. Arnold provides an excellent critique of Wink's position in his book *Power of Darkness*, 198-201. Arnold states: "I believe that he commits a methodological error known as an 'illegitimate totality transfer'. This error occurs when a total series of relations in which a word is used in the literature is read into a particular case. Each context must determine the range of possible meanings which are appropriate to that context." Ibid., 198. Further, Arnold disagrees with Wink that the biblical writers had both the human and spiritual powers in mind when using the terms.

[155] Cullman comes to the same conclusion as Wink, based on his exegesis of the term '*exousia*' in Rom. 13:1. He contends that the term *exousia* "means both the invisible 'princes of this world', who are often mentioned as such, and their actual human instruments." Oscar Cullmann, "The Subjection of the Invisible Powers," in *Engaging the Enemy*, ed. C. Peter Wagner (Ventura, CA: Regal Books, 1991), 193f.

[156] Green, 84-86; Arnold, *Powers of Darkness*, 200; and Clinton Arnold, *Ephesians: Power and Magic* (Grand Rapids: Baker Books, 1989), 129-34.

a functional interaction between the earthly structures and the demonic powers. It is an interaction in which the powers exert their rule, power, and authority through influencing the structures to exert their authority in an ungodly manner.

The Existence of a Demonic Hierarchy

Scripture affirms a hierarchy among the demonic forces but does not speculate on its exact nature. It clearly states that Satan commands the demonic forces and rules over the demonic kingdom (Mark 3:22-30; Luke 10:17; Rev. 12:9). However, Scripture does not speculate about the exact nature of the hierarchy. It focuses on the function and purpose of the powers and does not classify or analyze them.

In the current Spiritual Warfare Movement, there is a trend to interpret the terms as a hierarchical systematization of the demonic forces. White suggests such a hierarchy based on Eph. 6:12.

> It is reasonable to assume the authority structure here [Eph. 6:12] is arranged in descending order. Daniel 10:13 and 20 unveil the identity of the *archai* as high level satanic princes set over nations and regions of the earth. The word *exousia* carries a connotation of both supernatural and natural government ... Presumably, the *dynamis* operate within countries and cultures to influence certain aspects of life. The *kosmakratoras* are the many types of evil spirits that commonly afflict people, e.g., spirits of deception, divination, lust, rebellion, fear, and infirmity. These, generally, are the evil powers confronted and cast out in most deliverance sessions. Even among them there is ranking, the weaker spirits subservient to stronger ones.[157]

The rationale for the classification is twofold. (1) Classifying the powers was a common practice among first-century Judaism and was a well-established practice among the church fathers. It is assumed that Paul was familiar with

---

[157] Thomas B. White, "Understanding Principalities and Powers" in *Engaging the Enemy*, ed. C. Peter Wagner (Ventura, CA: Regal Books, 1991), 61f. It is interesting to note that the various classifications differ from one another. In some cases they are contradictory. Larry Lea's classification of the terms, compared with White's proposed hierarchy points out this inconsistency. Lea classifies the powers as "1. Principalities. These are individual demon spirits. 2. Powers. This group includes the captains of teams of spirits (such as Legion in Mark 5:9). 3. Rulers of darkness. This group includes regional spirits. 4. Strongmen. These dominate wickedness in high places and oversee the other levels of demonic activity." Steven Lawson, "Defeating Territorial Spirits," in *Engaging the Enemy*, ed. C. Peter Wagner (Ventura, CA: Regal Books, 1991), 37f.

these classifications an included them in his references to the demonic powers. (2) Many who are active in deliverance ministry report that there are different levels of demons and powers.[158]

Page, Arnold, and Rohrbach do not believe that the biblical terms show a hierarchy. Page points out that "speculation about the names and ranks of evil spirits and the realm over which they rule is not only without biblical foundation, it is foreign to the spirit of the Bible."[159]

Various features of the power terminology underscore this point. (1) Hans Rohrbach believes there is not enough scriptural information contained in the terms to construct a sensible hierarchy. „Es ist müßig und bringt nichts, aus den Angaben der Bibel eine Rangordnung der Geister zu konstruieren. Sie sagt darüber zu wenig, also brauchen wir davon nichts."[160]

(2) The biblical terms, for the most part, are interchangeable. Arnold states, "there is no special meaning to each of the terms that would give us further insight into the demonic realm. The terms appear to come from a large reservoir of terminology used in the first century when people spoke of demonic spirits."[161]

(3) The different listings and diverse combination of the terms do not show a consistency in ordering the terms. The listings are intended to speak of the powers as a collective whole. The primary focus of the passages in which the lists are given is not to classify or analyze the powers, but to show Christ's supremacy over the powers.

Even though Scripture does not provide a hierarchy, it does provide some general insights into the nature of the demonic breakdown. It shows that not all demonic powers are the same. They differ according to their nature, disposition, purpose, function, position, and jobs. Hans Rohrbach states: „Sie (die

---

[158] Most of the experiential information comes from the disputed practice of interviewing the demons during deliverance ministry. Kraft supports this practice as a means for gaining valuable information about the demonic realm. Charles Kraft, *Defeating Dark Angels* (Ann Arbor, MI: Servant Pub., 1992), 157-75. One needs to question the wisdom of speaking with the demonic as well as question the reliability of the information that is received. For a dialogue on this issue, see Priest, Campbell, and Mullen, 26-31 and Charles H. Kraft, "Christian Animism or God-Given Authority?" in *Spiritual Power and Missions: Raising the Issues*, ed. Edward Rommen (Pasadena, CA: William Carey Library, 1995), 117-20.

[159] Page, 270.

[160] Rohrbach, 88.

[161] Arnold, *3 Questions*, 39.

Geister) unterscheiden sich nach ihrer Wesensart und ihren Aufträgen, ebenso nach ihrer Rangordnung in der Hierarchie Gottes."[162]

The Demonic Powers and Patron Angels of Nations

Scripture suggests a relationship between the demonic powers and people groups. Finger and Swartley, as well as Page, conclude in their study on the demonic in the Old Testament that the references to the demonic spirits show a close relationship between the nations, their rulers, and their gods and the demonic powers.[163]

In Scripture, the term 'nation' usually refers to a group of people who were united by blood ties or a common culture. In some cases, the group is associated with a specific territory or government rule. In this paper, the term 'nation' is understood as a group of people united by a common culture, who may or may not share a common territory.[164]

Through a combination of texts, the demonic powers are associated with patron angels of the nations. Deut. 32:8 states that 'sons of God' have been assigned to each nation. Most scholars agree that the expression 'sons of God' refers to spiritual beings.[165] They assume that these entities functioned as patron angels (Angels of Nations). The view proposed in Psalm 82 that the spiritual beings are responsible for the administration of justice in particular nations coincides with the concept of patron angels in Deut. 32:8. Gen. 6:1-4, Psalm 82, and Isa. 24:21-22 imply that some of these patron angels are in rebellion to God and are demonic.

Scripture implies that the angels of the nations and gods of nations are the same.[166] The references to gods in Deut. 32:17 and Ps. 106:37-38 imply and in Ps. 96:4-5 distinctly state that the gods are associated with certain nations. A widely held view of Isa. 24:21-22 suggests that the spiritual powers function as patron angels.

---

[162] Rohrbach, 87.

[163] Page, 81; Finger and Swartley, 17.

[164] *The Zondervan Pictorial Encyclopedia of the Bible*, s.v. "Nations," by J. Rea. Also see Dayton and Fraser, 118-20.

[165] Page, 43-54.

[166] Page points out that even though one can argue that the Old Testament references to heathen gods are actually references to natural beings, there is compelling evidence that the gods are suprahuman beings and are associated with the concept of patron angels set forth in Deut. 32:8. Ibid., 54-59, 66-68.

The passages in the Book of Daniel are the clearest indication that the demonic powers function as patron angels. Dan. 10:13, 20-21 and 12:1 associate spiritual beings, who are in rebellion to God, with certain nations (Persia, Greece, and Israel).

The New Testament does not address the concept of patron angels as such, but the New Testament language of the powers clearly shows that the demonic powers were rulers who had legitimate authority over set dominions, which includes nations.

The Association of Demonic Powers with Individuals and Structures of Power

The ancient worldview as well as scripture associates the demonic powers with those individuals who had power. Isa. 24:21-22 suggests that the spiritual powers were allied with the kings. Rabbinical tradition and the early church fathers attributed the evil characteristics associated with the kings of Babylon and Tyre in Isaiah 14 and Ezekiel 28 with the Devil and the demonic powers. Even though it is not directly stated, it is assumed that the demonic powers worked through the leaders and rulers of Jewish society, especially the Pharisees, in order to turn the people against Jesus and crucify him. As was stated above, the twofold usage of the New Testament language implies a functional relationship based on the common power characteristics.

The powers also functioned through opinion leaders. Jesus associates Peter with Satan in Matt. 16:23. Peter was an opinion leader and a close friend of Jesus. It can be assumed that Satan tried to use Peter's influence to keep Jesus from fulfilling his mission.

Social and ideological structures are also associated with the demonic in Scripture. The powers make use of the rituals, structures, and beliefs, which are related to the local gods and their worship. This would explain why God placed such an emphasis on destroying all aspects and objects of pagan worship when entering the promised land (Exod. 23:24; Deut. 12:29; Lev. 18:24). The New Testament relates the false teachings and ideologies to the demonic. It can be concluded that earthly gatekeepers and the related structures are subject to demonic influence and control.

The Demonic Powers Associated with the Collective Social Values of Society

The relationship of the gods to the demons in Scripture implies that the society's collective values, including cultural themes, are associated with the demonic powers. Emile Durkheim suggests in *The Elementary Forms of the Religious Life* that a society is inclined to worship itself. The society's values, ideals, and themes are wrapped up in the form of a person, animal, or object, which function as gods and are worshipped. For Durkheim a society's gods are a reflection of the society itself.[167]

This concept, when applied to the gods in Scripture, allows for a correlation between a society's social values, ideals, and cultural themes and the gods of the nations, whom Scripture identifies with the demonic powers.[168] As a result, the demonic powers can be perceived as entities, which reflect a society's themes and values. The cultural themes are not equated with the powers, but are associated with the demonic powers as they manifest themselves in the form of the nation's gods. Based on the various associations between the demonic powers, gods of the nations, and a society's values and themes, this study concludes that there is a functional relationship between cultural themes and patron angels of nations.

Summary

Scripture teaches that there are demonic, independent, personal spiritual beings who interact with the natural world. They affect and exert their influence over individuals, social networks and their rulers, structures and geopolitical territories. There is hierarchy among the powers, but Scripture is for the most part silent about its breakdown. Scripture addresses the powers as defeated, disarmed, and under the lordship of Jesus Christ, but who currently still influence nonbelievers, pose a threat to Christians, and hinder the work of missions. The powers are associated with the patron angels and the gods of the pagan nations who have become in many cases the focus of a nation's worship. Based on this relationship, it is possible to associate the powers with cultural themes. It is reasonable to conclude from Scripture that there is a functional relationship between the powers and social networks and its structures, as well as an association between the powers and cultural themes which functions to keep humans blinded to the gospel and hinders the advancement of missions.

An Analysis of Current Interpretations of the Powers/Theme Relationship

Since World War II, there has been a growing interest in the demonic powers and their relationship to structures. Various theologians and missiologists have begun to debate the role powers play in the establishment and maintenance of

---

[167] Emile Durkheim, *The Elementary Forms of the Religious Life* (New York: Free Press, 1965), 970-72.

[168] Deut. 32:17, Ps. 96: 5, and Ps. 106:37 associate demons with the gods worshipped by the pagan nations.

society's evils and their influence on missions. This field of study has been labeled "Strategic-Level Spiritual Warfare" and is an integral part of the overall Spiritual Warfare Movement. Since the 1990s, it has significantly influenced the way missions are conceived, planned, and practiced. The current proponents of strategic-level spiritual warfare have approached the topic from two directions.

The Theological-Ethical Approach

The focus of the theological-ethical approach is on the demonic powers' relationship to social ethics. It relates the 'Principalities and Powers' in the Pauline writings to the evil structures prevalent in today's society (e.g., power structures, governments, companies, laws, ideologies, religious structures, traditions, etc.). Many theologians such as Hendrikus Berkhof, Walter Wink, and Rudolf Bultmann demythologize the powers and equate them with the earthly structures. Others, including John Linthicum, and Michael Green, maintain the existence of personal supernatural beings, yet stress the close association of the powers to the structure. The goal of this approach is to restore the demonic structures to their proper function. Addressing and bringing change to the structures themselves overcome the demonic powers. Social and political activism is the most important tools used. This approach has had significant effects on the ecumenical movement through the works of Walter Wink. Most of the proponents have either a New Testament or ethics background.

The Evangelistic Approach

The focus of the evangelistic approach is the demonic powers' influence on evangelism and missions. The interest in the demonic lies primarily in the desire to increase the effectiveness of evangelism and missions by successfully dealing with the powers. Most of the proponents of this approach affirm the presence of real, independent, personal demonic beings which influence structures, institutions, social networks, and geopolitical territories in order to blind groups of people to the gospel. The structures are restored through casting out or limiting the influence of the demonic powers. The primary tools of this approach include warfare prayer and power and truth encounters. Most representatives are missiologists and include C. Peter Wagner, Timothy Warner, George Otis, Clinton Arnold, Tom White, Charles Kraft, and Paul Hiebert.

This approach has become the driving force in evangelical missions. At the 1989 Lausanne II conference in Manila, strategic-level spiritual warfare was a widely discussed topic. In the 1990s, it has become an integral part of many mission curricula in seminaries and mission training schools. The most visible global mission strategy in evangelical circles, the 2000 A.D. movement, has incorporated many strategic-level spiritual warfare concepts. In 1989, a number of missiologists, theologians, and ministers joined together to form the loosely knit working group known as the 'Spiritual Warfare Network'. Its purpose is to serve as a forum for discussing spiritual warfare issues as they relate to world evangelization. Strategic-level spiritual warfare concerns are becoming a more integral and accepted part of Christian theology, ethics, missions, and ministry.

Worldview Presuppositions

Various views on the nature of the demonic powers have emerged within the Spiritual Warfare Movement. These diverse views have been shaped and conditioned by the interpreter's presuppositions. The most significant of these is a person's worldview. Those in the Spiritual Warfare Movement have tried to establish assumptions and premises that integrate the biblically based supernatural view of reality with the scientific realities and developments of the twentieth century. The resulting worldviews range from an exclusive materialistic, scientific worldview to differing expressions of the supernaturally based view of reality.

Those holding to a materialistic, scientific worldview adhere to a dualistic view of reality. They make a clear distinction between the natural and supernatural worlds and suppose little to no interaction between the two dimensions. Cause and effect are explained in exclusively scientific terms. As a result, the references to the demonic powers in Scripture are demythologized and reinterpreted. Hiebert refers to this position as 'modern dualism'.[169]

Those holding a supernatural worldview affirm a three-tiered system of reality. The "transempirical-other-world" level includes a God who has created and controls the universe as well as all the supernatural forces and beings. The "empirical-world-of-senses" level includes all aspects of the visible, natural world. The "middle zone" is the invisible dimension, which includes those supernatural forces, which reside and function in the natural world. These beings include the Holy Spirit, angels, demons, and other supernatural forces. The supernatural worldview assumes that there is a continuous interaction between the "middle zone" and the "empirical world."[170]

In an attempt to establish a biblical understanding of the "middle zone", a number of questionable views have developed. Some of these reflect more of

---

[169] Paul G. Hiebert, "Healing and the Kingdom," chap. in *Anthropological Reflections on Missiological Issues* (Grand Rapids: Baker Books, 1994), 219.

[170] Paul G. Hiebert, "Flaw of the Excluded Middle," chap. in *Anthropological Reflections on Missiological Issues* (Grand Rapids: Baker Books, 1994), 196-98.

an animistic worldview, a New Age view of reality, or the Indo-European worldview rather than a biblical view of reality.

A central issue of the Spiritual Warfare Movement is to discover and integrate the biblically based view of reality into Christian thinking and ministry.[171] This study affirms the supernatural view of reality, as presented in Scripture, and assumes a perceivable and continuous cause and effect relationship between the supernatural and natural worlds.

A Suggested Taxonomy of the Views of the Powers/Structure Relationship

This study proposes a division based on the different views of how the powers relate to structures.[172] Up until recently, most theologians in the twentieth century who have dealt with the demonic powers have equated them with the sociopolitical structures in human societies. Recently, a number of theologians and missiologists have returned to the traditional model, which associates the powers with structures, but do not equate them with each other. Based on these two basic positions, four models have emerged: the demythologizing model, the dependent model, the independent model, and the interdependent model.

The Demythologizing Model

The majority of theologians who adhere to this model assume that the references to supernatural beings in Scripture were vestiges of the outdated, antique worldview, which needs to be demythologized by one method or another. Rudolf Bultmann states: "Now that the forces and the laws of nature have been discovered, we no longer believe in spirits, whether good or evil."[173]

The demonic powers mentioned in Scripture are demythologized and equated with the negative forces associated with psychological, social, cultural, political, or religious structures or institutions. They are created by deeply rooted social sins such as oppression, greed, racism, pursuit of power, and other

---

[171] The term "biblical view of reality" is preferred to that of "biblical-worldview" or "Christian-worldview". The Bible does not present one cohesive worldview. It is written with a consistent view of reality which has been integrated into a Hebrew, Greek, and other ancient contexts. It would be incorrect to label either the Hebrew or Greek worldview as the Christian worldview. Kraft, *Christianity and Culture*, 349.

[172] For other taxonomies, see C. S. Lewis, *The Screwtape Letters* (New York: Macmillan, 1982), 3; O'Brien, 110-50; and Thomas H. McAlpine, *Facing the Powers: What Are the Options?* (Monrovia, CA: MARC, 1991).

[173] Rudolf Bultmann, "New Testament and Mythology," *Kerygma and Myth: A Theological Debate*, vol. 1 (London: SPCK, 1964), 10.

forms of collective evil. Once generated, they often go beyond the control of humans and establish an independent identity. The powers are engaged through this worldly means such as sociopolitical interaction or the establishment of contrast societies. The goal of engagement is to redeem the power structures. The process theologian, Daniel Day Williams, sums up the basic position of the demythologizing model as follows:

> We recognize the reality of demonic modes of experience and forms of power without committing ourselves to belief in demons as supernatural beings flying about the world at the command of an archfiend, one of whose names is Satan. Rather, we are seeking to understand the demonic as an experienced mode of action; it enters our human history with describable efforts.[174]

Representatives include Martin Dibelius, Rudolf Bultmann, Gordon Rupp, and Daniel Day Williams.[175]

This model takes the demonic phenomena seriously, but fails to acknowledge the spiritual dimension of the powers. They function within the confines of their western, scientific worldview and interpret the powers in light of their presuppositions, rather than reflecting the scriptural view of reality. Their portrayal of the powers as sociopolitical structures does not correspond with the biblical understanding of the powers, nor does it do justice to the historical context of Scripture, which affirms both the existence of a spiritual realm and the reality of independent, supernatural beings.

The Dependent Model

This model acknowledges the demonic powers as a spiritual force, but still identifies the powers with the structures. The powers are seen as internal spiritual forces that underlie sociopolitical structures, institutions, or ideologies. The spiritual and natural dimensions of the powers are dependent upon each other and cannot exist apart from each other.

The primary method of engagement is sociopolitical action, nonviolent resistance, and the creation of a contrast society. Prayer is the primary means for dealing with the power's spiritual dimension. The goal of the engagement is to

---

[174] Daniel Day Williams, *The Demonic and the Divine*, ed. Stacy A. Evans (Minneapolis: Fortress Press, 1990), 3.

[175] Martin Dibelius, *Die Geisterwelt im Glauben des Paulus* (Göttingen, Germany: Vandenhoeck & Ruprecht, 1909); Rudolf Bultmann, *The New Testament and Mythology and Other Basic Writings* (Philadelphia: Fortress Press, 1984); and Gordon Rupp, *Principalities and Powers: Studies in the Christian Conflict in History* (Nashville: Abingdon Press, 1952); and Williams, *The Demonic and the Divine*.

redeem the powers by reforming them to their intended purpose through the power of the gospel.

The most extensive treatment of the demonic powers to date is found in Wink's 'Powers' trilogy.[176] In his work he suggests that the powers are natural structures that are driven by an internal, supernatural, demonic force called the inner essence.

> The "Principalities and Powers" are the inner and outer aspects of any given manifestation of power. As the inner aspect they are the spirituality of institutions, the "within" of corporate structures and systems, the inner essence of outer organizations of power. As the outer aspect they are political systems, appointed officials, the "chair" of an organization, laws – in short all the tangible manifestations which power takes. Every power tends to have a visible pole, an outer form – be it a church, a nation, or an economy – and an invisible pole, an inner spirit or driving force that animates, legitimates, and regulates its physical manifestation in the world. Neither pole is the cause of the other. Both come into existence together and cease to exist together.[177]

Wink rejects the notion of an independent, personal spiritual being.

He suggests that these powers become demonic and idolatrous when they place themselves over God's purpose. The task of the church is to expose the powers and call them back to their created purpose according to Eph. 3:10. Both the outer and inner essence needs to be addressed. The outer essence is addressed through earthly means such as sociopolitical actions. The inner essence is changed through God's intervention. The Christian needs to engage in prayer and exercise faith in God, trusting him that he will change the spirituality of the structures. Even though Wink acknowledges and deals with the spiritual dimension, his emphasis is on the outer change since "it is precisely the outer changes we make that challenge, lure, and goad the oppressor toward inner change."[178]

---

[176] Wink, *Naming the Powers*; *Unmasking the Powers*; and *Engaging the Powers*.

[177] Wink, *Naming the Powers*, 5.

[178] Ibid., 122. Three problems of Wink's position need to be mentioned. (1) Even though Wink tries to create a biblical picture of the demonic, he has abandoned the biblical view of reality. (2) His dependent approach is based on the interchangeable use of the 'power' terminology in Scripture as was explained earlier. (3) He paints a more positive picture of the demonic powers, especially their futures, than is presented in Scripture. For an evaluation of Wink's work, see Arnold, *Powers of Darkness*, 198-201; and Nigel Wright, *The Satan Syndrome: Putting the Power of Darkness in Its Place* (Grand Rapids: Zondervan Pub., 1990), 43-50.

John Howard Yoder, in his *Politics of Jesus*, interprets the powers in the context of Christian social ethics and makes a similar interpretation. He acknowledges the literary meaning of the demonic powers, but sees the power preeminently in human structures, not independent of them. He interprets the powers primarily as political and economic structures. He advocates a "contrast society model" for dealing with the powers.[179] Other representatives include Hendrikus Berkhof, S. C. Mott, Ron Sider, Richard Mouw, and Oscar Cullmann.[180]

Even though the spiritual nature of the powers is taken seriously, this approach in practice continues to demythologize the powers and equate them with structures. There are three general problems inherent in this view. (1) There is no adequate explanation why structures sometimes become evil and at other times not. (2) The malevolent activity of Satan is restricted by this model. One can assume that the demonic powers' activity is not limited to structures. (3) Those who adhere to this model have a tendency to view the essence of society and structures as inherently evil, rather than affected by evil.[181]

The Independent Model

The powers are perceived as independent, personal, and spiritual beings. In comparison to the demythologizing and dependent models, the powers and structures are conceived as separate entities who are associated with one another, but independent of each other. The powers have remained the same throughout the ages and have operated and manifested themselves to the visible world in different ways at different times according to the beliefs of the people. Van Rheenen elaborates:

> My contention is that the essence of these powers, although taking different forms and manifesting themselves in different cultural ways, is the same for all ages. They are not merely socio-economic systems that have rebelled against God but personal spiritual powers opposed to the very

---

[179] John Howard Yoder, *The Politics of Jesus* (Grand Rapids: William Eerdmans Pub., 1972).

[180] Hendrikus Berkhof, *Christ and the Powers* (Scottsdale, PA: Herald Press, 1962). Stephen C. Mott, *Biblical Ethics and Social Change* (New York: Oxford University Press, 1982); Richard J. Mouw, *Politics and the Biblical Drama* (Grand Rapids: William Eerdmans Pub., 1976); Sider, "Christ and Power," 8-20; Cullmann, "The Subjections of the Invisible Powers," 193-202.

[181] Stott, 156. For further evaluations of this position and the various proponents, see P. T. O'Brien's article "Principalities and Powers," and Arnold Clinton, "'Principalities and Powers' in Recent Interpretation," *Catalyst* 17 (Feb. 1991): 4-5.

being of God. Although the names of powers who oppose God vary in different biblical contexts, their origin and essence are one.[182]

The powers are either dealt with through direct or indirect confrontation. Through dealing with the powers, the structures are changed. The focus of ministry is on the powers rather than the structures. Most believe that the structures should be saved, but not the powers. The primary goal of this model is to overcome the powers in order to increase the evangelistic harvest. This has been the predominant approach throughout Christian history and still prevails among nonwestern Christians as well as in western evangelical circles. Three representatives of this independent model include C. Peter Wagner, Clinton Arnold, and Paul Hiebert.

Wagner, the most visible 'Third-Wave' proponent of strategic-level spiritual warfare, views the demonic powers as independent, personal spiritual beings who can control people, structures, and territories. His focus is currently on the territorial spirits, who control and rule over geopolitical territories. A major emphasis of his position is that the powers operate within set geographic areas. He seeks to identify and name the powers through spiritual mapping. The goal is to cast them out of the territory through such means as confrontational warfare praying, identificational repentance, and power encounters so that the evangelistic harvest in the area will increase.[183] Others associated with Wagner's approach include George Otis, Jr., Cindy Jacobs, John Dawson, Charles Kraft, and Frank Peretti.[184]

---

[182] Gailyn Van Rheenen, *Communicating Christ in Animistic Contexts* (Grand Rapids: Baker Books, 1991), 101.

[183] C. Peter Wagner, *Warfare Prayer* (Ventura, Ca: Regal Books, 1991); *Breaking the Strongholds*; and *Confronting the Powers*. Wagner has become the lightening rod for the Third-Wave-oriented strategic-level spiritual warfare approach. His views have been criticized on a number of points. They include: (1) His worldview is closer to animism and the Indo-European worldview than the biblical view of reality. (2) His use of scripture is questionable. (3) He uses a faulty epistemology. (4) His approach overemphasizes the demonic powers. (5) There is a tendency to overemphasize methodology. (6) Wagner's approach is characterized by excessive pragmatism. (7) His concept of "territorial spirits," is oversimplified and naive. For critical reviews of Wagner and the Third-Wave approach, see Priest, Campbell, and Mullen; Wolfram Kopfermann, *Macht Ohne Auftrag* (Emmelsbüll, Germany: C & P Verlag, 1994); and Hiebert, "Healing and the Kingdom," and "Spiritual Warfare." For a rebuttal see Kraft, "Animism or Authority?"; and Wagner, *Confronting the Powers*.

[184] Dawson, *Taking Our Cities*; George Otis, Jr., *The Twilight Labyrinth* (Grand Rapids: Chosen Books, 1997); Frank Peretti, *This Present Darkness* (Westchester, IL: Crossway Books, 1986); Kraft and White, *Behind Enemy Lines*; and Cindy Jacobs,

Chapter III: Relationship of Demonic Powers to Cultural Themes

Arnold represents a more balanced approach to the demonic. He agrees with Wagner that the powers are independent spirits who stand behind the earthly structures and who need to be overcome. He principally agrees that the powers can be tied to geographic areas, but he, as well as others, has distanced themselves from this emphasis. His focus is primarily on the relationship between the spiritual powers and social structures.

Arnold advocates an indirect approach to dealing with the powers. The powers are indirectly engaged by appealing to Christ either to limit or cast out the powers. Once personally confronted with the powers, the believer has the authority to exorcise the powers. He and others have tried to combine the 'resist' and 'exorcism' motif in their approach to dealing with the powers.[185] Others who share Arnold's viewpoint include Tom White, Timothy Warner, and John Robb.[186]

Hiebert agrees with Arnold and Wagner as to the independent and spiritual nature of the powers. He associates the powers with cultural and religious structures rather than territorial areas. Wagner and Arnold promote an aggressive and power-oriented approach in dealing with the powers, but Hiebert believes that the Bible calls for a more resistance-oriented approach. He promotes a "shalom"-oriented model of engagement which emphasizes the way of the cross, where Jesus defeated the powers through submission rather than through a show of power.[187] Others advocating this approach include John Powlison and Nigel Wright.[188]

The strength of the independent model is its strong emphasis on the supernatural nature of the powers. It stresses the spiritual side of evil and provides a biblical view for dealing with the demonic threat. A danger inherent in this model is its tendency of overspiritualizing the powers. This has led some to focus on the spiritual dimension of the problem and to ignore the earthly dimension.

Possessing the Gates of the Enemy (Tarrytown, NY: Chosen Books, 1991).

[185] See Clinton Arnold's works *Ephesians: Power and Magic*; and *3 Crucial Questions on Spiritual Warfare*.

[186] Tom White, *Breaking Strongholds* (Ann Arbor, MI: Servant Pub., 1993); Warner, *Spiritual Warfare*; and John Robb, "Satan's Tactics for Building and Maintaining His Kingdom of Darkness," *International Journal of Frontier Missions* 10 (Oct. 1993): 173-85.

[187] Hiebert, "Healing and the Kingdom"; "Spiritual Warfare" and Hiebert and Shaw, "The Power and the Glory".

[188] Wright, *The Satan Syndrome*; and John Powlison, *Power Encounters* (Grand Rapids: Baker Books, 1995).

The Interdependent Model

The interdependent model is a synthesis of the dependent and independent models. The interdependent model goes a step further than the dependent model and views the earthly structures (or individuals) and the demonic powers as separate entities. Van Rheenen states that the powers are seen as "actively impacting the socioeconomic and political structures of societies, but at the same time being personal entities."[189] In contrast to the independent model, this model views the relationship between the powers and structures as interdependent. The powers are inherently tied to the structures by manifesting themselves through them to the visible world. The powers cannot be known by the visible world apart from the structure with which they are associated. The structure and powers are independent entities, but when it comes to knowing and dealing with the powers, they are tied to the structure.

There is a difference of opinion concerning the fate of the powers. Some believe that the evil powers will be restored to their former state, while others believe that they will be eventually destroyed. All agree that the structures are to be redeemed and restored to their intended purpose.

The powers are to be confronted in the context of their manifestation on both the supernatural and the natural levels. On a supernatural level, the powers need to be resisted and overcome through truth and allegiance encounter. On occasion, there is a need for power encounters. On a natural level, the Christians need to resist and stand firm against the evil associated with the structures as well as seek to transform the structures through this-worldly means such as sociopolitical activities, holy living, contrasting lifestyle, love, etc. Representatives of this view include Michael Green and Robert Linthicum.

Green argues that the powers are independent spiritual beings, who are separate from structures yet dwell within the structures. The powers are located there where they can influence people. Green points out that there are various evil features within modern society and the Christian church, which suggest the presence of supernatural evil forces.[190]

In dealing with the powers, Green notes, "the spiritual and social aspects of the gospel of Christ are inseparable."[191] He lists five ways to respond to the demonic threat. Through watchfulness, resistance, prayer, boldness, and involvement, Christians are to transform the earthly structures and confront the

---

[189] Van Rheenen, 101.

[190] Green, 99-111.

[191] Ibid., 234.

powers that lie behind them. By dealing with the earthly structures on both natural and supernatural levels, the powers are defeated.

Robert Linthicum, head of the World Vision's Office of Urban Advance, deals with the powers in the context of urban ministries. He agrees with Wink that the powers are the inner essence of the structure, yet they are also personal and independent. When the structures cease, the powers remain. In the context of city life, Linthicum explains the relationship of the powers to structures as follows:

> The political system of a city is infused with a spiritual essence; a "soul" unimagined and unexplored inner depths. This angel of a city is the inner spirituality that broods over that city. And that spirituality has immense power – either for good or ill.[192]

The means for engagement is closely tied to the amount of knowledge one has of the powers. Knowledge and engagement are closely related. Linthicum suggests becoming informed about the nature, function, and strategy of the powers to deal properly with them. The awareness of the nature, purpose, and function of the powers dictate the tools and objectives of engagement.

The strength of this view is that it provides a way to maintain the independence of the powers, yet show their close relationship to the structures without equating them. Furthermore, it takes the spiritual nature of the powers seriously, yet shows the importance of dealing with them in this earthly context. The powers are associated with earthly structures and need to be dealt with as natural entities. However, the spiritual dimension of the powers plays a significant role in dealing with the powers and structures. This view does not allow for an overspiritualization of the powers, or the overemphasis of the natural dimension. This view tries to keep a balance between the spiritual and natural dimensions of the powers without identifying one with the other.

Summary

The various positions are significantly shaped by the interpreter's worldview presuppositions. The four models show the spectrum of views on the nature of the demonic powers. The main difference between the models is their understanding of how the powers relate to structures. The demythologizing and dependent models equate the powers with the structures. The independent and interdependent models associate the powers with the structures. The demythologizing and dependent model overcomes the powers by transforming the structures. The independent model transforms the structures through dealing

---

[192] Robert C. Linthicum, *City of God, City of Satan* (Grand Rapids: Zondervan Pub., 1991), 115.

with the powers. The interdependent model calls for both addressing the powers and transforming the structures as the means to overcoming the powers' influence. All the models seek to save the structures. The demythologizing, dependent, and some representatives from the interdependent model believe that the powers need to be saved as well. The independent model does not seek to save the powers. The analysis of the relationship to structures in Scripture and the current views on this issue will provide the basis for the following Powers/Theme Relationship Model.

A Suggested Model for the Powers / Theme Relationship

The biblical analysis shows that there is a functional relationship between the demonic powers and cultural themes. The current interpretations of the demonic powers agree that there is a relationship, but differ as to its nature. How can the insights gained from the previous two analyses be applied to cultural themes in the context of missions? This section will suggest a conception model which will show the nature of the demonic powers/theme relationship and the impact the resulting demonic strongholds have on the individual, his or her society, and their attitude toward the gospel.

The Nature of the Powers / Theme Relationship

The biblical analysis has shown that there is a cause and effect relationship between the spiritual world and the natural world, as well as between the demonic powers and the visible structures of power. The previous chapter has shown that cultural themes are ideological structures of power, which shape people's lives. Based on these two assumptions and the correlation between the gods of a nation with the society's values and core themes, it can be assumed that the demonic powers associate with cultural themes and use them for their purposes.

Based on the previous analyses, the study assumes that the powers/theme relationship is interdependent. Cultural themes are ideological structures, which exist in the minds of the people and influence and control people through habit, social controls, and their use by cultural gatekeepers. The demonic powers are independent, personal spiritual beings of power. The demonic powers relate to the themes and distort them by influencing and shaping the gatekeeper's and the society's understanding and use of the themes. The powers use the power and control mechanisms associated with the themes to hold people captive to a distorted view of reality and the gospel. The powers are not equated with the themes or the gatekeepers, but manifest themselves and function in the visible world through the themes and their related gatekeepers. In the visible world, the powers can only be known and engaged within the context of their earthly manifestation, which includes cultural themes.

In America, the theme of individualism has shaped and conditioned the thinking and behavior of the American society. Associated with this theme are demonic powers that through individual and corporate sin have distorted the concept of individualism and use it for their rebellious purposes. Through key gatekeepers, the force of habit, and the various control mechanisms in society, the powers have integrated the distorted understanding of individualism into the American cultural matrix. The more distorted the understanding of individualism becomes; the more the American society is blinded to the full message of the gospel. The powers are not equated with individualism or with the structures, institutions, and gatekeepers who promote individualism. They are interdependently associated with each other. The demonic powers manifest themselves in and function through the society's understanding and practice of individualism.

The Purpose of the Demonic Powers

The original purpose of all created beings and structures is to worship and bring glory to God. The original purpose of the powers is to glorify God by serving as an instrument of power, which sustains, upholds, and protects God's creation from falling into chaos. As a result of their fall, the powers are using their God-given power to rebel against God. In conjunction with human sin, they use people and structures, such as themes and gatekeepers, to keep people and people groups from worshipping and glorifying God. They do this distorting and perverting all aspects of creation, interjecting their evil and destructive ways, and turning people's worship to themselves.

The powers continue to pursue their original function of sustaining, upholding, and protecting God's creation from chaos, yet they pursue it independently from God and his principles. Berkhof illustrates this point well by stating that the powers unify people, yet separate them from God.

> The state, politics, class, social struggle, national interest, public opinion, accepted morality, the ideas of decency, humanity, democracy – these give unity and direction to thousands of lives. Yet precisely by giving unity and direction they separate these many lives from the true God; they let us believe that we have found the meaning of existence, whereas they really estrange us from true meaning.[193]

---

[193] Berkhof, 26.

The goal of the demonic is to keep as many people as possible captive to a distorted view of reality and blinded from God's redemption and true worship. Through cultural themes, the demonic forces can exert their influence over a large number of people and keep them in 'collective captivity'.

The Nature of the Demonic Powers' Influence on Cultural Themes

The Relationship between Powers, Themes, and Humans

Kraft and Pennoyer believe that cultural systems, structures, and themes are "manipulated and controlled by demons acting through individuals."[194] Kraft points out that demonic control is always over people, not over a structure or structural system. Through people, the powers gain control and distort structures, but are not associated with them. "When a cultural subsystem seems to be controlled by Satan, it is really the group that operates that subsystem that is controlled. It is the people, not the subsystem itself, that need to be delivered from the demons."[195] Kraft makes a strong argument that demons associate with and function through individuals not structures.

His view is a helpful reminder that the powers/theme relationship is played out within human beings. Kraft is right when he states, "satanic control is, therefore, over a society, a people. It is not over a culture, a structured system."[196] The powers work through people and gatekeepers to shape and use the themes, however, observations and experiences show that structures, ideas, or cultural themes can become so dominant and controlling that they take on an identity of their own. They become an independent force that exceeds human control. At this state, the demonic powers associate themselves with the themes, which manifest themselves and function through human beings.

The Demonic Influence through Cultural Gatekeepers

The demonic powers affect and distort cultural themes through influencing people's understanding and use of the themes. The focus of the powers is the cultural gatekeepers associated with the themes. Through the gatekeepers, the demonic powers reshape and distort the themes and maintain the distortion in the society.

---

[194] Pennoyer, "Dark Dungeons," 256.

[195] Charles H. Kraft, "In Dark Dungeons of Collective Captivity: Response by Charles H. Kraft," in *Wrestling with Dark Angels*, ed. C. Peter Wagner and F. Douglas Pennoyer (Ventura, CA: Regal Books, 1990), 274.

[196] Ibid., 275.

The powers gain access to the gatekeepers and the themes through the corporate sins of the group or the individual sins of the gatekeepers. It has been shown that sin opens the door for demonic activity. Sinful group decisions, which compromise the theme's original purpose, provide the demonic powers access and the resources to reshape the content of the themes. Sinful activity of the cultural gatekeepers allow the powers to manipulate the gatekeeper's understanding, expression, and use of the theme, thus affecting the rest of the people. Once the distortion has been established, it is strengthened and maintained through continuous sinful activity.

When the themes are distorted, their original purpose, which is to glorify God, is replaced. Through the distortion, the themes and the associated gatekeepers and structures become the center of worship. The powers maintain the original function of the theme. A theme that does not meet basic needs of the group will be rejected. However, it is important to note that the longer the themes are distorted and controlled by the powers, the less they are able to fulfill even their basic functions. At this point, the society will seek to transform or change the themes. Either the demonic forces will establish new distorted themes or the community of believers can restore the themes to their original God-given expression.

Through the themes, the powers influence the cognitive, emotional, evaluative, and motivational dimensions of people's lives. The powers use the themes to create distorted principles for individuals to live by. They use experiences to create an emotional attachment to the distorted themes. The powers coordinate a string of events and situations, which establish a bond of allegiance between the distorted themes and the people. The result is a collective captivity, a spiritual stronghold centered on the demonic distortion. Pennoyer describes it as follows:

> The combined activity of demonized individuals, leading others in traditionally demonic focused activities, creates collective captivity. Individuals sit in collective captivity in their dungeons in the common societal prison surrounded by the collective darkness created by this demonic permeation of their cultural system.[197]

The demonic distortion creates theme-related demonic strong-holds, which keep a society captive to a distorted view of reality.

---

[197] Pennoyer, 257.

The Nature of Theme-Related Demonic Strongholds

A Definition of "Demonic Strongholds"

The interaction of the demonic powers with cultural structures, such as cultural themes, produces demonic strongholds.[198] A demonic stronghold is defined as an entrenched pattern of thought, value, or behavior, which is contrary to the will of God and has been erected through the combined efforts of the demonic influence and human will. They are the place from which and through which the demonic powers operate.[199] The powers' influence on cultural themes creates theme-related demonic strongholds, which keep individuals and groups captive to a worldview and a cultural pattern, which is in conflict with the cause of Christ.

Human sinfulness and the demonic powers work together to create these demonic strongholds. White states:

> As Paul depicts in 2 Cor. 10:3-5, the stronghold exists within a person, but is traceable to and exploited by satanic forces ... Our culture is littered with demonically inspired values and ideologies such as intellectual cynicism, hedonism, greed, racial pride, and hatred ... I believe Frank Sinatra's biographical song "I Did It My Way" exposes one of our more glaring cultural strongholds: the idolatry of individualism. Such ways of thinking and living may emanate from the human heart, but satanic forces can also manipulate them.[200]

The strongholds originate through human sin and develop through the influence and coordination of the demonic powers. They become the base from which the powers operate and launch their activities.

---

[198] Structures are defined as sociological, ideological, and cultural elements which make up a society's integrated cultural system, determine the characteristics of a society, and function as the glue that holds a society and its culture together. They influence and control how individuals and groups organize their lives and determine how the social, intellectual, and spiritual life of a group functions. It includes such things as symbols, ideologies, behavior and thinking patterns, institutions, beliefs, norms, values, worldview assumptions, cultural themes, etc. Cultural themes are understood as ideological structures. Hermann Amborn, "Strukturalismus: Theorie und Methode," in *Ethnologie: Einführung und Überblick*, ed. Hans Fischer (Berlin: Dietrich Reimer Verlag, 1992), 337f.

[199] White, *Strongholds*, 24; George Otis Jr., *Strongholds of the 10/40 Window* (Seattle: YWAM Pub., 1995), 8.

[200] White, *Strongholds*, 24.

Types of Demonic Strongholds

Gary Kinnaman identifies three types of demonic strongholds. (1) Territorial strongholds are geographic territories that are under the control of territorial spirits. Much of the current strategic-level spiritual warfare literature deals with territorial strongholds. (2) Ideological strongholds are assumptions, worldviews, values, ideas, philosophies, and religious beliefs that influence individuals and their society's thinking and behavioral patterns. Theme strongholds fall into this category. (3) Personal strongholds are thoughts, attitudes, and behavioral patterns within the individual that keep the person captive to sin and rebellion. These strongholds are part of ground-level spiritual warfare. This study will focus on the ideological strongholds.[201]

The Origin of Theme-Related Demonic Strongholds

Pennoyer suggests a model explaining how the demonic strongholds are created in a society.[202] His model will be used to illustrate the manner in which theme-related strongholds evolve. There are four phases.

The Distraction Phase

The demonic powers distract the individual or group from their God-given path, function, or purpose. They will cause an event or circumstance to come up which questions the validity of the theme. This may be an outside threat to the society, a new innovation, an unexplainable event, etc. The leaders of the group are faced with the challenge of responding in light of their established cultural themes.

The Deception Phase

The group, or the gatekeepers, will reaffirm, restate, reformulate, or redefine the cultural theme to fit the challenge. At this point, the demonic powers try to distort the situation and present a distorted formulation, expression, or use of the original theme, which gives the appearance of adequately solving the problem. In most cases, it will involve compromising the original purpose and function of the theme. The new distorted theme will always be coupled with a sinful action, decision, or agreement.

---

[201] Gary D. Kinnaman, *Overcoming the Dominion of Darkness* (Old Tappan, NJ: Chosen Books, 1990), 54-60.

[202] Pennoyer, 266-70.

The Dependency Phase

Once the distorted theme is planted in the minds of the gatekeeper and the people, the themes become more and more part of the thinking process of the people. It is incorporated into the cognitive, emotional, evaluative, and motivational dimensions of their lives. In many cases, the themes will become absolutized as well as the center of worship.

The Domination Phase

The themes become more dominant within the society. At this stage, the powers/theme relationship becomes a demonic stronghold. The powers are associated with the themes and their expressions and are able to exert control through the themes' natural control mechanisms. With the help of the themes, the powers are able to establish a theme-based resistance to the gospel. As the themes are established and become an integral part of society, their grip is harder to overcome.[203]

When the validity of the distorted themes is once again challenged, this process repeats itself, establishing a new demonically distorted theme. In conjunction with this cycle, corollary strongholds are created that strengthen the major theme. The demonic powers are responsible for coordinating this process and maintaining and strengthening the strongholds.

The strongholds are maintained through the natural control mechanisms associated with the themes (pull and press forces). The powers create and transform symbols, forms, structures, and institutions through the distorted themes. They use intimidation, distraction, manipulation, seduction, enticement, and fear of alienation to keep people conformed to a distorted view of reality.

Characteristics of Theme-Related Demonic Strongholds

The various theme-related strongholds display several common features.[204]

(1) The cultural themes of the demonic stronghold become absolutized and sanctified. It is the common belief that the demonic powers attack at the weakest point. But in many cases, if not most, the powers associate themselves

---

[203] At this stage it appears that the distorted themes have become determinative. As was pointed out in the last chapter, neither the themes nor the powers can take complete control over people. There is always some part of the human will empowered by the Holy Spirit that can resist and overcome the influencing power of the themes and the powers.

[204] These features are based on Daniel Day William's presentation of the demonic in *The Demonic and the Divine*, 7-14.

with the strengths of a society, sanctifying and absolutizing this cultural element. Williams states: "We see further that to find the demonic in social structures, we should look to the most sanctified and powerful forms of culture, not because sanctity and powers are demonic in themselves, but because these are the forms through which the demonic invade."[205]

As the themes become absolutized, they become the focus of the society's worship, requiring the people to give their complete allegiance to the themes or those objects and people associated with the themes. They reject all other possible theme expressions or anything that conflicts with the distorted themes. They become the absolute criteria or principles for ordering and evaluating the areas of life addressed by the themes.

(2) The demonic stronghold creates a false drive and fascination. The powers use the cultural themes to cast a spell over individuals, releasing passionate energies and motivating them under the guise that the themes will set them free.

(3) The demonic stronghold maintains a distorted view of reality. All areas of life become distorted. Pleasure and fear, good and bad, right and wrong, what is important and unimportant, all are distorted. There is a deviation from the basic doctrines of Christianity.

(4) The demonic stronghold creates a vacuum in the life of the people. New needs emerge that are temporarily, but inadequately, fulfilled by the distorted themes.

(5) The demonic stronghold creates an independent system of control with its own momentum. A form of legalism evolves to protect the themes and their stronghold. The themes control the society, rather than serving the society.

(6) The distorted themes in the demonic stronghold begin to provide purpose and direction for the society. They direct the society away from their God-intended purpose and vocation.

(7) The demonic stronghold creates a false sense of security. The society is deceived into thinking that the distorted themes will provide for all their needs. This false sense of security creates closed-mindedness and intolerance to other ways.

The Influence of Theme-Related Strongholds on Missions

The theme strongholds create thinking patterns, attitudes, reasoning processes, and criteria of evaluation that establish a hostile environment for the gospel. It is important to be aware of the missiological significance of the themes, the demonic powers, and the related strongholds. Many churches and mission

---

[205] Ibid., 6.

agencies focus exclusively on the individuals and fail to see the importance of the cultural structures. This allows the powers to maintain their control over the culture and individual through the theme strongholds. In order to reach people, one must deal with individuals as well as the cultural themes, the demonic powers, and the strongholds, which keep individuals captive.

The strongholds are broken through Christ's power and authority. The basis for the authority is the cross. On the cross, Christ defeated the demonic powers. Even though they still exert their power of distortion and deception, they are subject to Christ's authority. Through the cross, everyone is able to escape the grip of Satan's captivity.

The life, death, and resurrection of Christ provide the power and strategy for breaking the stronghold. Jesus' life was focused on breaking spiritual, cultural, and sin strongholds in individuals and the Jewish society. He sought to change individuals and society through transformational encounters. Jesus encountered the demonic powers and set people free from their captivity through power encounters. He continually encountered the Jewish gatekeepers (Pharisees and other Jewish leaders) and engaged them in truth encounters. He preached God's kingdom, which entailed the original understanding and use of the Jewish law. He continually challenged people to undergo an allegiance encounter.

The cross was the ultimate encounter. God demonstrated his power through love, truth, and suffering. He did not challenge the powers with a show of power, but by exposing the powers' distortions. On the cross, the powers were exposed for who they were and the strongholds broken. It opened the door for people to restore their relationship with God through Christ.

Through transformational encounters, the demonic powers will be overcome, the cultural themes restored, and the strongholds broken. It will allow people to see and hear the gospel for what it is. The themes will become the means by which people come to know Christ, rather than being the source of hindrance. Dealing with the demonic strongholds will be dealt with in more detail in chapter 5.

Conclusion

This chapter has shown that there is a functional, interdependent relationship between the demonic powers and cultural themes. The powers work through structures and cultural themes, distorting them from their original expression and function in order to create theme-oriented demonic strongholds, which keep people and groups captive and blinded to the gospel. The second part of the study will explore possible means for dealing with these strongholds. It will focus on identifying the themes through spiritual diagnosis, a form of spiritual mapping, and confronting the theme strongholds through transformational encounters.

Chapter IV
Spiritual Diagnosis

Introduction

The first section of the study deals with the nature of cultural themes and the impact of sin and the demonic powers on their context, expression, and use. The previous chapters show that the demonic powers blind people to the gospel by distorting and using the themes for their purpose, thus creating demonic strongholds. The following two chapters will focus on the practical dimensions of the theme-related demonic strongholds (theme strongholds) and will develop a strategy for dealing with them.

The process is divided into two phases: the research phase and the strategy phase.[206] Chapter 4 will focus on the research phase in which the spiritual condition of the group is diagnosed and evaluated. It identifies the cultural themes, the demonic powers, and the resulting strongholds. The strategy phase evaluates the research results and creates a plan of action. It establishes the goals and the procedures for engaging and overcoming the strongholds. Chapter 5 will deal with the various aspects of creating such a strategy.

Understanding the problem is the first step in solving the problem. In order to deal with the demonic stronghold, it is necessary to have an in-depth knowledge of the situation. It is important to identify the themes, know their redemptive purpose, discern any possible distortions, as well as recognize the various powers and forces, which exert control over the themes. An in-depth and complete diagnosis of the target group will lead to a more focused strategy and more efficient ministry.

The purpose of this chapter is to establish a diagnostic research model that will identify the cultural themes, the controlling powers, and the related demonic strongholds, through combining ethnographic, ethnohistorical, and sociological research with spiritual discernment. This type of research has come to be known as 'spiritual mapping'. The chapter will begin by analyzing and evaluating this current concept. Based on this analysis, the study will propose a revised spiritual-mapping approach, called spiritual diagnosis, which focuses on theme strongholds. The goal of the chapter is to show how a combination

---

[206] Robb, *Focus*, 39. The study affirms the need for scientific research in missions. For discussion on the place of research in missions, see Charles Kraft, *Anthropology*, 459-67.

of scientific research and spiritual discernment can help identify the cultural themes and their related strongholds in order to create an appropriate strategy.

An Analysis of Spiritual Mapping

In the early 1990s, a new form of research called spiritual mapping emerged as part of the Strategic-Level Spiritual Warfare Movement, which combines social research with spiritual discernment in order to increase the effectiveness of missions. It has developed as a mission's tool in response to two realizations: (1) The traditional methods of research are insufficient for understanding all the forces that hinder the spread of the gospel; (2) there is an increasing awareness that demonic powers play a key role in frustrating evangelistic efforts. As a result, many have turned to spiritual mapping in order to understand better the spiritual dimensions of the target group and territory they are evangelizing. This research method is becoming more and more popular, especially within the Third Wave Movement.[207]

What is spiritual mapping? This section will analyze and evaluate the concept of spiritual mapping and the different approaches and practices associated with it. This analysis will provide the basis for setting up a spiritual diagnosis model that will help in identifying the theme strongholds.

A Definition for Spiritual Mapping

George Otis, Jr. coined the term 'spiritual mapping' in reference to the emerging systematic approach of identifying the spiritual powers, their activity, and influence within a given area. He defines spiritual mapping as "superimposing our understanding of forces and events in the spiritual domain onto places and circumstances in the material world." It does not manipulate or create reality,

---

[207] Most of the leading proponents of spiritual mapping are associated with the Third Wave Movement. They include C. Peter Wagner, George Otis, Jr., Cindy Jacobs, Bob Beckett, and John Dawson. Currently, a limited number of works have appeared on this subject. They include: Wagner, ed., *Breaking the Strongholds in Your City*; Dawson, *Taking Our Cities for God*; George Otis, Jr., *The Last of the Giants* (Tarrytown, NY: Chosen Books, 1991); Otis, *The Twilight Labyrinth*; and Bob Beckett, *Commitment to Conquer* (Grand Rapids: Chosen Books, 1997). George Otis, Jr. has also published a how-to-manual on Spiritual Mapping. George Otis Jr., *Spiritual Mapping Field Guide: North American Edition* (Lynnwood, WA: Sentinel Group, 1993). Mansfield, *Releasing Destiny* is an example of a spiritual mapping project. In most cases, spiritual mapping is treated as a subtopic within the various works on strategic-level spiritual warfare. Wagner commits two chapters on spiritual mapping in his book *Warfare Prayer*.

but it sees the situation as "it really is, not as it appears to be."[208] Harold Caballeros compares spiritual mapping to an X-ray, which goes beyond the visible dimension to determine the invisible sources and causes of a problem. "Spiritual mapping gives us an image or spiritual photograph of the situation in the heavenly places above us."[209]

Spiritual mapping discerns, through in-depth research, the events and forces in the spiritual realm that keep people within a given area or cultural group from responding to the gospel. It combines anthropological, sociological, and historical research with spiritual discernment to bring to light the spiritual condition of a region, city, nation, or people group. It seeks out relevant data concerning the identity of the demonic forces as well as their methods and strategies through which they influence the people of the target area. The basic objective of spiritual mapping is to establish a spiritual profile of the area or group targeted for evangelism.

Spiritual mapping is objective in that it can be verified or discredited by history, sociological observation, and God's Word. It is subjective in that it is based on spiritual discernment and a right relationship with God. The main critique of spiritual mapping centers on the validity and reliability of spiritual discernment.

The concept developed out of a need for more relevant information so that the evangelistic efforts and strategies can become more focused and effective. In the past, research has focused on the natural, visible dimension of a situation. But based on the assumption that there is a discernable cause and effect interaction between the natural and supernatural world and the belief that the demonic powers use geopolitical, social, cultural, and ideological structures to blind people to that gospel, the research has expanded to deal with the spiritual realm. It has taken a whole new dimension into account for creating evangelistic strategies.

There is a similarity between the place of spiritual mapping and the new developments in general geographical mapping. Advancements in technology have opened the mapper to dimensions of the physical earth that are invisible to the eye, yet play a significant role in understanding the earth's geography. *The National Geographic* article "Revolution in Mapping" by John Noble Wilford points out that new developments have revolutionized mapping. The most significant has been the developments of techniques that have allowed

---

[208] Otis, *The Last of the Giants*, 85.

[209] Harold Caballeros, "Defeating the Enemy with the Help of Spiritual Mapping," in *Breaking the Strongholds in the City:*, ed. C. Peter Wagner (Ventura, CA: Regal Books, 1993), 57.

the mapper to consider important influences on the mapping process that are invisible to the eye.[210]

The same impact these new techniques have had on map making, spiritual mapping has had on understanding the barriers to evangelism. Causes not visible to the natural eyes are now being detected by spiritual mapping, helping evangelism and intercession become more focused and, as a result, more effective.

Current Understandings of Spiritual Mapping

In the early stages of spiritual mapping, a diverse number of research projects appeared which greatly differed in quality, objectives, and methodologies as well as in the basic understanding of the spiritual mapping concept.[211] As the mapping concept has matured and become a more integrated part of mainstream mission strategies, a common understanding and standardized approach to mapping has emerged. Presently, three general directions to spiritual mapping exist.[212]

The Powers-Oriented Approach

The focus of this approach is on researching the nature and identity of the powers. It is built on the assumption that the more knowledge a person has of the powers, the more able he or she will be to overcome and cast out the powers. C. Peter Wagner advocates this view.[213] His primary focus is on identifying and naming the territorial spirits. Spiritual mapping is the first step in exorcising the demonic powers. For Wagner, the goal of spiritual mapping is to identify the territorial spirits, to know their distinct nature and character, and to map out the area of their control and authority. Spiritual discernment is emphasized over the other forms of research.

---

[210] John Noble Wilford, "Revolution in Mapping," *National Geographic* 193, no. 2 (February 1998): 13.

[211] In recent years, the basic understanding, the methodologies, and the acceptable standards of quality have become more and more standardized through the work and leadership of George Otis, Jr. As a leading proponent of spiritual mapping and coordinator of the Sentinel Group and the Spiritual Mapping Division of the United Prayer Resource Network, a division of the AD 2000 Movement, he is currently establishing a center for spiritual mapping which is working on developing spiritual mapping research standards. Louis Bush, ed., *AD 2000 and Beyond Handbook* (Colorado Springs: AD 2000 and Beyond Movement, 1993), 19.

[212] Spiritual mapping is an integral part of the 'AD 2000 and Beyond Movement', one of the largest and most extensive global mission strategies for world evangelization.

[213] Wagner, *Warfare Prayer*, 143-60.

Two distinguishing features of this approach are 'naming the powers' and 'mapping out the geographic boundaries of their authority'. (1) The primary goal of spiritual mapping is to know as much as possible about the powers which includes knowing their names. Wagner and others highly recommend finding and knowing the names of the territorial spirits when doing strategic-level spiritual warfare. Wagner states:

> We need to recognize that those who deal regularly with the higher levels of the spirit world agree that, while knowing the proper names might not be necessary, it is helpful in many cases. The reason is that there seems to be more power in a name than many of us in our cultural might think.[214]

Clinton Arnold questions this practice. He points out that even though Scripture speaks about territorial spirits, there is little to no information given about their activity and organization, nor is there a mandate for identifying, naming, or confronting them. He does not reject the territorial spirit concept, but questions the importance and value of identifying, naming, and engaging the territorial powers as is called for by many spiritual warfare advocates.[215]

He further argues that this practice is based on the faulty assumption that if you can somehow get the name of the demonic ruler, then you have more power over it. This was a common assumption in antiquity and is still prevalent in many animistic religions. When looking closely at the New Testament treatment of the powers, it is precisely this kind of mind-set that Paul was speaking against when he reaffirmed to the Ephesians that Christ's position was "far above all rule and authority and power and dominion, and every name that is named" (Eph. 1:21). The power to overcome the demonic is in knowing Christ, not in knowing their identity or names.[216]

(2) Another defining aspect of this approach is identifying and mapping out the exact boundaries of the powers' jurisdiction. Wagner believes the spirits are assigned to geographic territories, which can be discovered through mapping. He proposes a form of mapping which draws lines connecting the various religious constructs, occultic centers, and areas of increased crime and sin in order to indicate the demonic corridors of power. As a result, the geographic boundaries of the demonic powers can be charted and their center of powers exposed. Knowing their names and charting their boundaries of influence provide the needed information for effectively engaging the territorial spirits.

---

[214] Wagner, *Warfare Prayer*, 150, 176.

[215] Arnold, *3 Crucial Questions*, 161.

[216] Ibid., 163.

The Manifestation-Oriented Approach

The focus is on the nature of the powers' manifestations. By knowing the nature of the manifestation, the power-related strongholds can be identified and overcome. This approach is associated with George Otis, Jr.[217] He shares the same basic views concerning territorial spirits and spiritual mapping as Wagner, yet differs in his emphases. In comparison to Wagner, Otis is more concerned with how the powers have manifested themselves in an area or group and the nature of their deception rather than identifying the powers themselves. The objective of spiritual mapping is to profile the spiritual condition of a city or an area through careful research. In contrast to Wagner, Otis stops short of trying to identify and name the demons or map out their boundaries of influence.

A second difference in his approach is his emphasis on the scientific research aspect of spiritual mapping rather than the spiritual discernment aspect. Otis places a high priority on quality and verifiable research. Spiritual discernment directs or verifies the research, rather than being the major source of new information.

The Culture-Oriented Approach

This approach focuses on the powers and their manifestations in social networks and their cultures. Tai M. Yip suggests this alternative approach in his article "Spiritual Mapping: Another Approach."[218] He distances himself from the territorial spirit concept. He suggests that spiritual mapping is not dependent on the territorial spirit concept, as some have suggested. Rather than defining the demonic strongholds by their geographic boundaries, he suggests viewing the strongholds in a context of social networks and their cultures. The cultural approach provides the basic framework for the spiritual diagnosis model presented below.

An Evaluation of the Approaches

The three approaches have the same basic understanding of spiritual mapping, but differ in their emphases and methodologies. The first two approaches are based on the territorial spirit concept. Wagner seeks to identify the spirits; Otis

---

[217] George Otis, Jr., "An Overview of Spiritual Mapping," in *Breaking the Strongholds in the City*, ed. C. Peter Wagner (Ventura, CA: Regal Books, 1993), 29-47; and Otis, *Spiritual Mapping Field Guide*. Another representative of this approach is Clinton Arnold, *3 Crucial Questions*, 175-77.

[218] Tai Ming Yip, "Spiritual Mapping: Another Approach," *Evangelical Mission Quarterly* 31 (April 1995): 166-70.

focuses more on the nature of their influence. In contrast to Wagner and Otis, Yip suggests a spiritual mapping model that is independent from the territorial spirit concept.

The methodologies reflect the model's basic disposition. First, Wagner relies more on spiritual discernment for information. Otis and Yip use spiritual discernment more as a confirmation and interpretation tool. Second, Wagner's goal is to identify and cast out the demonic spirits. Otis and Yip are concerned about understanding the nature of the power's influence as well as overcoming it. This may or may not include casting out the spirits. All three approaches affirm the importance of researching the spiritual dimension of a territory or social network in order to increase the effectiveness of doing missions.

An Evaluation of Spiritual Mapping

The presence of spiritual mapping raises some important questions. The most important concerns the mandate for spiritual mapping. The first section of the evaluation will analyze the biblical mandate for spiritual mapping. The second section will look at the benefits and dangers of spiritual mapping.

A Possible Biblical Mandate for Spiritual Mapping

There are no direct references in Scripture to the current form and practice of spiritual mapping. However, there are references that imply or suggest the practice of spiritual research in Scripture. There are three arguments used by proponents in establishing a biblical basis for spiritual mapping.[219]

(1) Spiritual mapping is a logical response to such verses as Eph. 6:10 and 2 Cor. 2:11. Eph. 6:10 points out that there are demonic powers who are responsible for hindering the advancement of the gospel. According to 2 Cor. 2:11, Paul does not want his readers to be ignorant of their devices and schemes. This last verse does not only refer to a general understanding of Satan's devices, but also includes knowing and exposing Satan's strategies for specific situations. Spiritual mapping is the tool, which provides both general and specific knowledge about Satan's schemes.

(2) Various Old Testament passages refer to spying out the enemy and surveying the land in preparation for battle. Num. 13:1 and Josh. 2:1 report that spies were sent into the promised land to survey the situation before it was to be invaded. Josh. 18:8 reports that the land was surveyed in order to divide the land among the tribes of Israel. According to the spiritual mapping proponents, the same tasks, which Israel conducted in the natural realm, can be implemented in the spiritual realm. When entering a territory that is occupied by

---

[219] Otis, *Field Guide*, 15.

demonic forces, the area should be surveyed and profiled before the enemy is engaged.

(3) There are two passages that imply spiritual mapping activity in scripture. (a) In Ezek. 4:1-3, the prophet is instructed by God to make a map of Jerusalem and to depict the coming siege on the city. It was a portrayal of the spiritual state of Jerusalem. (b) Acts 17:16-34 implies that Paul surveyed the city in some form, observing the local sites and customs thus gaining an understanding of the spiritual state of the city before addressing the crowd at the Areopagus. The information he had gained guided his evangelistic appeal.

These Scripture references imply, but do not specifically state or promote spiritual mapping in Scripture. There are indications spiritual research was practiced, but there is no direct precedence. Therefore, it is wrong to speak of a biblical mandate. Without a precise biblical precedence and mandate, should spiritual mapping still be practiced?

Otis differentiates between something being extrabiblical and unbiblical. He states, "Extrabiblical is a yellow light that encourages passage with caution; unbiblical is a red light that requires travelers to halt in the name of the law and common sense."[220] The only reason that spiritual mapping may be viewed as unbiblical is that Jesus and his disciples neither practiced spiritual mapping nor instructed others to seek out information about the spiritual realm. At the same time, there is no mandate in Scripture, which forbids this type of research. Spiritual mapping is an extrabiblical tool that should be used with caution. Wagner compares it with the Sunday School concept. It is not biblical, but it has proved to be a valuable tool for evangelism and church growth.[221]

Spiritual mapping is foremost based on logical reasoning and pragmatism, rather than on a biblical precedence. The same logic and pragmatism that encourages the use of sociological and anthropological research in the Church Growth Movement is used to justify spiritual mapping. Just as sociological research helps identify sociological barriers hindering church growth and evangelism, spiritual mapping identifies spiritual barriers. Spiritual mapping is the logical consequence and a necessity for those dealing with the spiritual influences on evangelism and the church growth process. Even without a clear biblical mandate, spiritual mapping should still be used with caution based on its logical necessity, general biblical principles, and its proven pragmatic usefulness.

---

[220] Otis, "Spiritual Mapping," 35.

[221] C. Peter Wagner, "Introduction," in *Breaking the Strongholds in the City*, ed. C. Peter Wagner (Ventura, CA: Regal Books, 1993), 20.

Benefits of Spiritual Mapping

There are a number of ways in which Spiritual Mapping has proven helpful. It benefits intercessors and mission strategists by providing more accurate and in-depth information for their prayer and evangelism efforts. It brings to light the underlying spiritual causes for the visible condition of an area. The new information is helping intercessors to focus their warfare praying, and it is providing mission strategists needed information for allocating their resources more effectively. The 10/40 Window, a concept widely used by intercessors and mission strategists, is a product of spiritual mapping. Other benefits include helping create more contextualized methods for sharing the gospel and discipling new Christians. It also provides a needed guide for contextualizing theology in various societies.[222]

Dangers of Spiritual Mapping

There are some dangers and concerns that are associated with the current understanding and practice of spiritual mapping.

(1) Current spiritual mapping has a tendency to overemphasize the demonic powers. This is the major concern voiced by most critics of spiritual mapping and spiritual warfare.[223] On the whole, this criticism is valid. Much of the literature, rhetoric, and practice of current mappers reflect an overemphasis on the power and threat of demonic beings and an underdeveloped theology of God's sovereignty and the power of the cross. Wagner acknowledges this danger. "Uncovering the wiles of the devil can become so fascinating that we can begin to focus attention on the enemy rather than on God. This must be avoided at all costs." However, in this context he also points out that it is important to have adequate knowledge of Satan's workings and strategies.[224]

This unbalanced focus is a major concern. However, it does not negate the place and use of spiritual mapping as such. It merely calls for balance and caution. Any research into the demonic domain needs to be coupled with a clear understanding of God's sovereignty and Christ's authority.

---

[222] Arnold, *3 Crucial Questions*, 177.

[223] The "Statement on Spiritual Warfare" by the Intercession Work Group of the Lausanne Committee for World Evangelization lists nine dangers associated with the current Spiritual Warfare Movement. The first two deal with the overemphasis or preoccupation with the demonic powers. The Intercession Working Group, Lausanne Committee for World Evangelism, "Statement on Spiritual Warfare," *Urban Mission* (December 1995): 51.

[224] Wagner, "Introduction," *Breaking Strongholds*, 22.

(2) Spiritual mapping has a tendency to overemphasize methods and techniques. Spiritual warfare and mapping tend to emphasize certain formulas and techniques in dealing with the demonic.[225] Even though research and methodologies are helpful, they cannot replace the spirit-guided ministry. The danger in spiritual mapping is that it is often pressed into a formula. At the same time, spiritual mapping has reintroduced the Holy Spirit into the area of research. Spiritual discernment and spiritual insights are essentials for Christian research.

(3) Many spiritual mapping projects tend to be subjective, speculative, and arrive at questionable and superficial conclusions. In some of the models, the subjective element dominates as the main source of knowledge. In other cases, mappers rely more on information gained through spiritual discernment and prophetic insights than on scientific research.

There is an inherent danger in using these sources of knowledge as the basis for establishing a cause and effect relationship. The integrity of spiritual mapping is based on a proper relationship between the subjective and objective research elements. It is important that the subjective impressions and information be verified and tested as well as being in harmony with other objective sources of information.

(4) Current spiritual mapping overemphasizes the territorial and geographic dimensions of the demonic activity. The current understanding of spiritual mapping is closely related to the concept of territorial spirits. Many of the spiritual mapping projects are based on the assumption that the demonic spirits are subject to geographically bound territories. The praxis shows that often there is a correlation between demonic activity and geographic sites and territories. However, these areas are always associated with human beings and shaped by social network boundaries.

Robb points out that there has been a shift from understanding communities (neighborhoods, cities, and nations) as social networks to perceiving them as geographic entities. As a result the demonic is no longer associated with people, but with geographic locations.[226] When a city is characterized by the sin of immorality, there is the danger that immorality is personalized and disassociated from human sinfulness. Humans become victims of immorality, rather than being responsible for its cause. It is important to remember that the demonic spirits work through people, not independently of them. Even though one cannot deny the fact that the powers are associated with territories, spiritual mapping should primarily focus on the relationship of the powers to indi-

---

[225] "Lausanne Statement," 51.

[226] Robb, *Focus*, 11.

viduals and groups of people. More work needs to be done in developing spiritual mapping models that focus on the various types of social networks. This would help in mainstreaming spiritual mapping and broadening its acceptance.

The evaluation of spiritual mapping indicates that there are some inherent dangers associated with the spiritual mapping concept and that there are some questionable views and practices associated with the popular understanding of spiritual mapping. At the same time, it indicates that spiritual mapping, when used correctly and with caution, has shown to be a helpful tool for evangelism and intercession.

The Spiritual Diagnosis Model

In light of the previous evaluation, this study suggests a model based on basic spiritual mapping principles, which is useful for determining the theme-related strongholds. The model differs from the current spiritual mapping approaches in its basic assumptions and goals. The basic position of spiritual diagnosis will be presented here.[227] The research process itself will be discussed in the following section.

Spiritual diagnosis, like spiritual mapping, is the research process, which combines sociological, ethnological, and historical research with spiritual insight and discernment, to create a spiritual profile of a defined group. It focuses on the manifestation and a phenomenon associated with the demonic rather than the powers themselves and analyzes the spiritual condition of the designated people group. It is similar to a medical diagnosis, which looks for the root cause of the illness in order to treat it properly. The spiritual diagnosis looks for both the natural and spiritual root causes for spiritual strongholds so that they may be overcome and the group's resistance towards the gospel broken.

The term spiritual diagnosis is preferred to spiritual mapping for two reasons. (1) As mentioned above, spiritual mapping is closely associated with the concept of territorial spirits and that of naming the powers. The proposed model is based on diagnosing the demonic manifestations in cultural groups and finding the cause for the related stronghold. In order to disassociate the research from the previous two concepts, the new term spiritual diagnosis will be used.

(2) The research is better described by the term diagnosis than mapping. Mapping implies locating the powers according to geographic location, whereas diagnosis associates the research process to a fact-finding investigation. The goal of this model is to profile the spiritual condition of the group, its themes,

---

[227] Arnold suggests this term as an alternate designation for spiritual mapping. Arnold, *3 Crucial Questions*, 187.

and the related stronghold. Through diagnosis, the root causes can be identified.

In this study, the concept of spiritual diagnosis will be applied to studying the theme strongholds. A spiritual diagnosis process will be presented through which the various natural and spiritual dimensions of theme strongholds and their impact on a society can be analyzed and evaluated using sociological, ethnological, and historical research combined with spiritual insights and discernment.

A Spiritual Diagnosis Model for Profiling Theme Strongholds

The following section will develop a diagnosis procedure that will identify the cultural themes and demonic powers and profile the related demonic strongholds. It will not present an in-depth, step-by-step manual, but will set up a general procedure for the research process. Some of the procedures are based on insights and procedures suggested in the *Spiritual Mapping Field Guide* by George Otis, Jr., the "Six Rules for Taking a City," by C. Peter Wagner, and the "Developmental Research Sequence Method" as presented by James P. Spradley.[228]

The research process includes three tasks. (1) It will address the important considerations in setting up the research, (2) it will analyze the different aspects of collecting and organizing the data, and (3) it will examine proper means for interpreting the data.

Setting up the Research

Determining the Target Group

It is important to pick a target group, which is small enough to manage, but big enough to have a missiological impact. The dimension of the task will have a direct bearing on the length of time the diagnosis will take. The group should either be a social group, societal group, or an association as was defined in chapter 2. If the group is small enough, the whole group can be the focus of the research. In the case of a large society (e.g., German culture), a representative group (e.g., the residents of a certain town or region) can serve as the research group. It is important to establish a task that is manageable.

---

[228] Otis, *Spiritual Mapping*, 17-53; Wagner, *Warfare Prayer*, 163-78; and Spradley, *Ethnographic Interview*, 227-34.

Second, the target group needs to be a social network of people, not a geographically determined group. Location is important in establishing the area where the research will be conducted, but the research itself needs to focus on one of the distinct people groups of that area.

Finally, when choosing a target group, it is important to know the nature of the group. Some groups have clearly defined boundaries. It is clear who belongs or does not belong. Other groups have blurred boundaries. The factor of association is not an external determinant, but an internal sense of belonging. Some identify closely with the group, whereas others see themselves as marginal members. Some groups have sharper boundaries than others.[229] Determining the size, nature, and type of the target group will help define the research, task, and goals.

Recruiting Outside Support

In any type of research project, there is the danger that the research becomes an end in itself. It is important that the information gained is applied. Since the goal of the diagnosis is to provide relevant information for the evangelism process, it is important to include initially those individuals and Christian groups who will be acting on the information. This has a number of benefits. It prepares those who will be ministering and builds their level of anticipation as the diagnosis develops. Sufficient and continuous communication between researchers and the implementers will help guide the research process and make it more efficient.

Setting up the Research Team

Spiritual diagnosis depends on a well-functioning and competent research team. Because of the nature and size of the task, the key to establishing this team is bringing together spiritually mature, motivated, and gifted individuals who are competent in the areas needed to accomplish the task.

Initially, it is vital to include and place people according to their talents and giftings. Otis states that there are three areas of research requiring people with specific giftings.[230] They include primary research, secondary studies, and spiritual discernment. The effectiveness of spiritual diagnosis is dependent on

---

[229] For discussion on the types of groups according to the nature of their boundaries, see Hiebert's discussion on typology of sets. He differentiates between bounded sets, intrinsic fuzzy sets, centered sets, and extrinsic fuzzy sets. Paul G. Hiebert, "The Category Christian in the Mission Task," chap. in *Anthropological Reflections on Missiological Issues* (Grand Rapids: Baker Book House, 1994), 110-33.

[230] Otis, *Field Guide*, 18-23.

placing the right people into the right units according to their giftings and talents.

An additional aspect of selecting a team is the inclusion of cultural insiders as co-researchers. There is the danger that the receptor culture becomes the object of research and is interpreted from an exclusive etic perspective.[231] Recently anthropologists and missionaries have found it helpful and essential to incorporate cultural insiders into the research process. They are able to provide a needed emic perspective to the process. Blending the insights of the outsider with the understanding of the insiders has been shown to produce a more in-depth and accurate understanding of the culture.[232]

Establishing Research Goals

Before one begins the actual research, it is important to have clear objectives and goals, as well as a clear overview of the scope of the study. Clear goals serve as a compass for the process and help eliminate unproductive research. Through the goals, the research remains relevant and applicable.[233]

The purpose of the cultural theme-oriented spiritual diagnosis is to provide an in-depth analysis of the cultural theme strongholds. It will provide relevant insights for transforming the cultural themes from strongholds of distortions to missiological tools. The goal is to identify the cultural themes, the spiritual forces responsible for their distortion, the gatekeepers who are presently controlling the themes, and their impact on society in order to establish a profile of the theme strongholds. During the study, it will become clear that there are a number of different strongholds affecting the society. It is important for the sake of the study to keep the research focused on one or two theme strongholds. Once these key strongholds are identified and properly confronted, the other strongholds will be easier to profile.

---

[231] The terms emic and etic are used by anthropologists to differentiate between the insider understanding and view of culture (the emic perspective) and the outsider's perspective (the etic perspective). The etic perspective is usually a comparative view, whereas the emic position provides the in-depth point of view. Hesselgrave, *Communicating Christ*, 124.

[232] Kraft, *Anthropology*, 469.

[233] Spradley suggests that the goals for any spiritual diagnosis should be built around the following three questions: What is the problem? What is the cause of the problem? And what are possible solutions to the problem? Spradley, *Ethnographic Interview*, 230.

Cautions and Dangers of Spiritual Diagnosis

There are dangers inherent in spiritual diagnosis that needs to be kept in mind. They include: (1) Ethnocentrism needs to be avoided in the research process. It is important to remain humble throughout the research process and maintain the right perspective, motives, and attitudes. This especially concerns the researcher's attitude towards the group under investigation. Often the missionaries and researchers are unwilling to respect fully the people and their culture. They study the people with a 'know-it-all' attitude, rather than learning from them. It is important that the researchers first become a learner before ministering or making judgments concerning a society.

(2) It is important that the research is balanced in its emic and etic perspective. Too often anthropological and spiritual mapping research is based on an etic perspective, ignoring the emic perspective, which results in a distorted profile. Both the insider's and the outsider's perspective are needed for accurate and complete research.

(3) Hasty decisions or prolonged research comprise the greatest danger for spiritual diagnosis. Often premature and simplistic judgments are made concerning the strongholds. Before conclusions are made, the data need to undergo a vigorous process of verification. Quality research and proper interpretation are essential for the success of the research process.

In contrast, there is the danger of not knowing when to stop. There are a number of interesting side issues that seem vital to the overall issue but usually are insignificant. Furthermore, there is always a need for more research. It is important to keep the goals in mind and make a conclusion once the information meets the set goals.

(4) Spiritual attacks are reported by most people involved in spiritual mapping or spiritual diagnosis. Wagner and others warn that it is important to maintain proper accountable relationships, prayer support, and personal integrity and holiness. Clearly, anyone who shakes the status quo or confronts the kingdom of darkness will need to be aware of and be prepared for spiritual attacks.[234]

The Research

Once the task has been defined, the objectives and goals set, and the research team put into place, the next step in the process is doing the actual research. Two questions need to be considered. What are the various issues that need to

---

[234] For a more detailed discussion on preparations for spiritual warfare see Wagner, *Warfare Prayer*, 105-23; and Otis, *Spiritual Mapping*, 57.

be researched? What are the appropriate means and methods for each of these research areas?

In order to meet the overall objective, which is to identify and analyze the group's theme strongholds, the research needs to focus on three tasks. (1) The themes need to be identified and the nature of their presence examined. (2) The forces of power that influence, control, and make use of the themes need to be unmasked and their relationship to the themes investigated. (3) The nature of the resulting strongholds needs to be analyzed and evaluated.

Basic Research Procedures

Before examining each of these research areas, the basic research approach needs to be defined. There are two basic sequences for doing research. Most social science research follows a chronological procedure: (1) Select the problem. (2) Formulate a hypothesis. (3) Collect the data. (4) Analyze the data in respect to the specific hypothesis. (5) Record the results.

An alternative procedure used in ethnographic research follows a cyclical sequence: (1) Select the problem. (2) Collect the cultural data. (3) Analyze the data. (4) Formulate an ethnographic hypothesis. (5) Record the results. The process requires a constant feedback and evaluation within each of the five phases. As a result the research process does not proceed chronologically, but rather cyclically. Researchers are at all stages simultaneously.

Spiritual diagnosis research is a mixture of both research models. On one hand, it sets forth the basic hypothesis that the theme strongholds are the cause for spiritual resistance. This hypothesis guides and directs the research process. On the other hand, the specific themes and the related strongholds are identified as a result of the above-mentioned ethnographic research. It is clear that themes and theme-related strongholds exist; their identity and nature, however, will emerge as the research progresses in a cyclical manner.

Understanding the Cultural Themes

The first task is to identify and analyze the group's cultural themes. It will include identifying the themes, their origin, their historical development, and their relationship to the gospel. The analysis consists of five steps.

(1) The first step is to identify the culture's major themes.[235] With the help of ethnographic interviews, participant observation and other related methodologies, which are discussed below, the content, expression, use, and emic under-

---

[235] Spradley provides a procedure for identifying cultural themes in his book *Ethnographic Interview*, 185-203.

standing of the themes are determined. The study should focus on the most dominant and influential theme. In order to keep the study manageable, only one or two themes should be analyzed. This is the most difficult and time-consuming step.

In conjunction with this step, it is important to determine the nature of the themes' influence on the group. How do they affect the cultural matrix of the group? What types of control mechanism do they work through? What are the counter-themes and how do they limit the influence of the themes? Do the counter-themes represent a channel for transforming the themes? Identifying the themes and understanding the nature of their influence lays the foundation for the diagnosis process.

(2) The themes are evaluated in light of biblical teachings. The content, expression, and use of the themes are compared to those biblical teachings and principles, which deal with the issues addressed by the themes. It is important to evaluate critically the themes from an emic understanding of scripture.[236] This comparison will enable the researcher to determine those areas in which the themes conflict with the gospel. This comparative analysis will provide insight into the identity and nature of the stronghold.

(3) The themes' original expression and redemptive purpose are identified. Once the nature of the relationship between the themes and the gospel has been determined, the next step is to identify the themes' original content and expression. It is important to analyze the difference between the current and the original expression of the themes in order to determine their spiritual purpose or redemptive gift. The study should also consider if Richardson's 'redemptive analogy' concept applies to the themes. This spiritual purpose sets the goal for the transformation process. It is more important in the ministry phase to know the redemptive purpose of the themes than to know the nature of the evil powers controlling them.[237]

(4) The themes' development from the original to the current state needs to be examined. The research needs to survey the historical development of the themes in order to understand the origin and nature of their distortion. Key events, group actions, and decisions, which have had a sig-nificant influence on the society and its themes, need to be identified and analyzed. These include such things as (a) events and decisions which led to the founding of the group; (b) the historical relationship between the group and Christianity; (c) events and decisions made in times of war, famine, and during other times of

---

[236] See Paul Hiebert's critical contextualization approach for the evaluation process. Hiebert, *Insights*, 186-91.

[237] Dawson, *Taking Our Cities*, 41.

national crises; and (d) continuous areas of conflict which have plagued the group. An overall history of the group will assist in locating and examining these events, decisions, and situations.

Through a historical study, it is possible to identify those past and present sins, which have contributed to the distortions of the themes. First, the most prevalent and current sins need to be identified. Often there will be one or more sins, which are more common than others and which characterize the group. In many cases, these sins are related to the themes. Either the sinful behavior is promoted and justified by the themes or the sins are expressions of the themes.

Second, it is important to identify past sinful decisions and actions of the group. Corporate sins, unholy alliances, ethical compromises, etc. often have redefined and subsequently perverted the themes' content in order to justify the group's actions. Defining these key events and decisions will help find those key factors leading to the distortions of the themes as well as the keys to breaking the strongholds. Dealing with these events and decisions is an important step in transforming the themes.

(5) The final step pulls the research together and makes a preliminary conclusion. It should show the ethnological cause and effect relationship between the major themes and the resistance of the people. This preliminary write up will help provide a framework for the following two research tasks.

Exposing the Powers Related to the Themes

The second task focuses on the powers, forces, and power structures associated with the themes. The research process needs to determine the overall power structure, the key gatekeepers, and the demonic powers which shape and are shaped by the themes. Once these forces are identified, the theme stronghold can be uncovered.

Spiritual diagnosis assumes the existence of both visible and invisible powers and a functional interrelationship. Both levels need to be investigated as they relate to the theme. The supernatural influences are exposed as a result of the diagnosis of the visible entities of power. The second task will first deal with the natural powers related to the themes and then turn to the demonic powers.

(1) The first step seeks to gain an overview of the existing power structures. Some of the key areas of investigation include the group's power hierarchy, the nature of their decision-making process, and the control mechanism used by the powers in charge. Both the formal and informal power hierarchies need to be considered. The real power often is located in the informal structures.

(2) The cultural gatekeepers need to be identified. The diagnosis seeks to determine those gatekeepers, which shape and are shaped by the themes. There

are two types of gatekeepers that need to be considered: the head gatekeepers and the local gatekeepers. The head gatekeepers are those who have influence over the group as a whole (e.g., presidents, kings, clan leaders, etc.). These leaders shape the belief system, values, direction of the group, as well as the content and expression of the themes.

The local gatekeepers have influence over a small segment of the society. They usually interpret the theme for the local setting and make sure that they are followed and maintained. Both types of gatekeepers need to be studied. When looking at the distortion of the themes, it is important to determine the responsible gatekeeper or gatekeepers.

(3) The gatekeepers' source of power needs to be determined. The gatekeepers' power may be based on their leadership quality, past success, achievements, wisdom, control over important resources (e.g., technology, natural resources, spiritual resources, etc.), status, position, or relationship to certain cultural structures. It is important in this context to determine the degree to which the themes empower the gatekeepers. In many cases, the themes serve as the base for their power. In other cases, the gatekeepers may use the themes to exert their power.

In conjunction with looking for the source of power, it is important to identify any past or present sins, which have established or maintained the gatekeepers' power and authority. It is through these sins that the demonic powers gain access to the cultural themes and are able to distort them. Both the personal sins of the gatekeepers as well as corporate sins of the group need to be considered.

(5) Once the natural gatekeepers have been identified and their relationship to the themes has been determined, the focus of the study should shift to the demonic powers. The diagnosis assumes that demonic powers are associated with the gatekeepers through the themes. The powers are identified through studying the themes and their various manifestations in the group. As was stated earlier, the diagnosis is not interested in identifying the identity or names of the demonic powers, nor will it set up a speculative characterization of the powers or the demonic world. Its interest in the powers is limited to the powers as they manifest themselves in the visible world through the themes.

Is it necessary, then, to refer to and talk about demonic powers? Realizing that demonic powers are an integral part of the distortion process helps in better understanding and dealing with the distortions. It is possible to overcome the natural dimensions of the distortion, yet fail to deal with the spiritual bondage that is related to the themes. As a result the transformation process is only superficial and does not adequately deal with the underlying cause for the theme's distortion, which is the demonic powers. Knowing the powers are at work and understanding the nature and form of their manifestation allows for a more focused and in-depth engagement.

(7) Finally, the diagnosis will show how the cultural themes, the natural gate-keepers, and the demonic powers relate. The goal is to determine how the demonic powers use the cultural gatekeepers to distort the cultural themes in order to keep a society or group captive. Once this relationship has been determined, it is possible to identify and profile the resulting theme strongholds.

Profiling the Cultural Theme Strongholds

The final task is to profile the theme strongholds. The strongholds keep the group captive on a cognitive, emotional, and evaluative level through the use of the themes. The diagnosis will profile the strongholds and their influence on each level by focusing on the nature of their influence and determining those structures and elements, which establish and support theme strongholds.

The first step is to look at the expression of the strongholds. The profile determines how the various destructive elements in the society relate to the themes. Some of these elements to be considered include the social ills of society such as injustice, poverty, or violence; the breakdown of cultural values, structures, and traditions; and the troubling trends in the society. The most prevalent and destructive expression is the groups' declared allegiance to and worship of the distorted themes. The themes are either directly responsible for these expressions of the strongholds or provide the basis for their existence.

(2) The second important area to investigate is how the strongholds are developed. When and how did the themes become strongholds? Using the distraction, deception, dependency, and domination cycle model presented in the last chapter, the distortion of the themes and the emergence of related strongholds can be charted. Two important areas to consider are the sins, which perpetuated the distortion and the events and circumstances through which the strongholds were birthed, developed, and strengthened. Secondary strong-holds, which support the theme strongholds, also need to be identified and profiled.

(3) The final step is to locate the potential areas for breaking the strongholds' power. The diagnosis needs to identify those power structures, which uphold the strongholds. These include the gatekeepers, cultural structures, rituals, values, customs, objects of worship, and other relevant cultural forms. These entities provide the power base for the strongholds. Identifying them will provide the first step in breaking the stronghold.

The three tasks will provide the needed information to identify the original and distorted expression of the themes; expose the influence of the demonic powers; create a profile of the strongholds and the spiritual condition of the group; and point out the starting point for transforming the cultural themes. In order to accomplish the three tasks and provide a working profile, certain tools and research methods are needed.

Methodologies

Spiritual diagnosis uses a variety of research methodologies for identifying the themes, exposing the powers, and profiling the strongholds. The first methodology, ethnographic interview,[238] is the primary method used by anthropologists for acquiring an in-depth understanding of the culture. In his book *The Ethnographic Interview*, James Spradley has developed a research procedure based on interviewing cultural informants and using various ethnographic questions for discovering a group's cultural themes. The interviewer builds a rapport with the informants in order to establish a framework for qualitative interviewing in which the informants can fully express their understanding of the culture and provide the researcher with a detailed map of the society and their cultures.

The advantages of the ethnographic interview are twofold. It not only provides information about the culture and its themes, but the informants also convey the feelings and emotional reactions that are associated with the different aspects of culture. In conjunction with the study of secondary sources, the interview helps clarify previous research as well as provide leads for more in-depth investigations. The major danger of this methodology is the tendency to transfer the views and feelings of one person on to the whole group. This is especially the case in interpreting the emotional impact themes and other cultural elements have on the group.[239]

The second methodology, participant observation, studies the cultural matrix of a group through observing and actively participating in as many parts of their cultural life as possible. There are two areas of observation: (a) people and their activities; and (b) culturally relevant places, institutions, and events. Both areas of investigation will help locate and define the cultural themes as well as help determine the level of spiritual bondage. Through observing the forms, duration, frequency, antecedent, and consequent patterns of the themes related to institutions, customs, rituals, myths, and other culturally important events, it is possible to discover the key themes.

---

[238] For a detailed description on conducting an ethnographic interview, see Spradley, *Ethnographic Interview*, 55-68, 78-91, 120-31, 155-71; Otis, *Spiritual Mapping*, 36-40; and Robb, *Focus*, 80-83. For a listing of types of questions that are useful and appropriate for interviewing, see Spradley, *Ethnographic Interview*, 223; and Otis, *Spiritual Mapping*, 59-66.

[239] Robb, *Focus*, 74-75.

The method is widely used by anthropologists for studying the belief systems of a society. Roy D'Andrade points out that

> at present, the most frequently used (and perhaps most effective) technique for the study of cultural belief systems is for the individual ethnographer to immerse himself in the culture as deeply as possible and, by some series of private, unstated, and sometimes unconscious operations, to integrate large amounts of information into an organized and coherent set of propositions.[240]

In his book *Participant Observation*, Spradley provides a step-by-step manual for conducting this method of research.

Even though this is the most effective ethnological research method, the time factor presents a significant drawback. For participant observation to be effective, it requires a significant block of time and a deep-seated commitment to become immersed into the culture. All those involved in spiritual diagnosis should anticipate the research phase to last a minimum of six months to two years.

Both methods work with primary sources, which may be human or structural sources.[241] Human sources are cultural insiders who serve as informants. They are an integral part of the group to be studied and have an in-depth knowledge about the various aspects of the culture. The key to interviewing is to find good and knowledgeable informants. Structural sources include culturally relevant institutions, customs, rituals, myths, and other important events and practices.

Participant observation and ethnographic interviews are most effective when they work together. Through interplay of these methods, the cultural code with its key themes can be deciphered and the related strongholds exposed. Both are essential for spiritual diagnosis. Observations help formulate questions and guide the interviewing process, and the interviewing process helps affirm observations and provide direction for further research.

---

[240] Roy D'Andrade, "A Propositional Analysis of U.S. American Beliefs about Illness," in *Meaning in Anthropology*, ed. Keith Basso and Henry A. Selby (Albuquerque: University of New Mexico Press, 1976), 155-80, quoted in James P. Spradley, *Ethnographic Interview* (Fort Worth, TX: Harcourt Brace Jovanovich College Publishers, 1979), 190.

[241] The overview of sources is based on Spradley's and Otis's discussion on the nature of good informants and sources. Spradley, *Ethnographic Interview*, 45-54; and Otis, *Spiritual Mapping*, 29-31.

A third methodology, secondary research, is an important part of research and draws on the study and knowledge of others. It is important to look for and search out existing sources relevant to the research. In many cases, the group has already been studied and written about. At the beginning of the research phase, these secondary sources should be surveyed. It will provide a general overview of the target group and help map out the research process. The more information that can be gathered at the preliminary stages, the easier the research will be. It is important to consider the material's point of view. Each analysis is made through the lenses of the writer's worldview. Resources include ethnographs, dissertations, travel guides, and written and visual documentaries.

Historical research, a fourth methodology, provides analysis and a foundation for doing the spiritual profile. Historical sources, which include written and oral materials (public records, personal letters and diaries, visual and literary art works, etc.), preserved artifacts and folklore, provide a direct insight into the historical development of the group, its culture, and its themes. These sources can provide insight into the original state of the themes, its current expression and use, as well as help identify the various influences that have shaped the themes. Any historical event or decision that has impacted the group's understanding and use of the theme needs to be researched further.

The fifth methodology, comparative approach, compares the various culture systems, by analyzing similarities and differences between the society's worldview assumptions and themes. The culture's themes are identified through the comparison process. The strength of this approach is that it allows the researcher to study the themes within a larger context. A drawback to the approach is its tendency to describe and define the themes in the researchers' etic terminology and categories. It is a supplementary research method.

The myths and rituals approach, a sixth methodology, provides one of the most insightful approaches for studying the themes. It analyzes the myths, rituals, and folklore associated with the group. In most cases, the underlying motif of the myths articulates the culture's themes. The rituals provide an insight into what values, norms, and allegiances are important to the society. The folklore of a society emphasizes those cultural elements and issues that lie at the heart of culture. Myths, rituals, and folklore help define and understand the themes. The analysis can occur through observation as well as through secondary research.

A seventh methodology, spiritual discernment, defines the various means by which divine insights are discerned. They include Scripture, divine guidance and words of knowledge, intuition, and information gained from direct contact with the demonic forces. The use and acceptability of each of these sources is dependent on one's worldview, biblical hermeneutic, and theological paradigm.

Otis suggests that the spiritual intercessors and other team members gifted in spiritual discernment keep a dated prayer log. Reoccurring themes and insights gained during their prayer times often provide guidance and help for the research process. They can be answers to questions raised by certain research challenges. It may provide guidance into new areas of research. It may be a spiritual interpretation of natural events.

Three general criteria need to be considered when including spiritual insights to the research process. (a) Extrabiblical revelation should be judged in light of Scripture. (b) The discernment process should be conducted by those with the appropriate gifting such as the gift of knowledge, spiritual discernment, or prophecy. (c) This source should be used with extreme caution. Because of its subjective nature and the high possibility of abuse, it should not become the primary or only source for key items of information. It should primarily serve to verify or dispel other sources of information. In some cases, divine insight will provide leads that need to be followed up and verified through other sources and other forms of research.

There are a number of different methods and sources available to spiritual diagnosis. The criterion for using these sources and methodologies is their ability to meet the basic objectives of discovering the cultural themes and helping understand the nature of the related demonic strongholds.

A variety of sources need to be used to attain a comprehensive picture of the situation. In order to assure the integrity and quality of the research, each source needs to be verified and crosschecked by the other sources. As various sources are consulted and the information mounts, it should establish a clear identity of the themes and provide a profile of the related strongholds.

Compiling the Data

The final step in the research phase is the sorting out and organizing the material. The better the organization the easier it will be to evaluate the findings and draw conclusions. Two aspects are important at this stage. (1) The research is to be well documented. (2) The organizing process is to begin from the very start of the study and continue throughout the research.

Pulling the Research Together

The final and most important stage in the research process is making the conclusions after analyzing and evaluating the compiled data.

Interpreting the Data

The interpretation process is similar to working on a large jigsaw puzzle. As the various pieces come together, the big picture becomes clearer. As the facts are organized and interpreted, the nature of the themes and their impact on society come into focus.

Spradley points out that researchers learn the culture and discover the themes by observing and listening to the people and then making inferences based on the received information. Since most cultural themes are implicit, they need to be determined through inference. Inference is drawing a conclusion from existing evidence or a set of premises through reasoning. "At first, each cultural inference is only a hypothesis about what people know. These hypotheses must be tested over and over again until the ethnographer becomes relatively certain that people share a particular system of cultural meanings."[242] Through inference, the facts lead the researcher to identify the themes and discover the relationship between the themes and the resistance of the people to the gospel. The result of the process is a clear diagnosis and profile of the theme strongholds.

There are some general cautions that need to be considered in this phase in order to complete the interpretation puzzle. (1) Any interpretation needs to be done with caution and with tentativeness. The results should always be open for reconsideration and modification. (2) The whole should never be interpreted on the basis of the particular. Core themes and key strongholds are often identified based on a limited research and selective sources. (3) The facts should speak for themselves. It is important to let the information and facts guide the interpretation process. Often researchers will try to interpret a presupposed hypothesis into the information. The themes need to emerge from the facts and not be based on preconceived notions.

(4) The data need to be weighed and evaluated. Five criteria should be considered: (a) Do the data come from an emic or etic perspective? Both perspectives need to be included in the interpretation process. (b) Are the data relevant to the overall objective? (c) How reliable are the sources? The integrity level of the sources determines the believability of the study. In the same light, it is important to know if information given by the sources is a statement of fact or opinion. (d) To what extent have the various facts been confirmed? Facts and information that reoccur throughout the research process are more likely to be accurate than information that appears only once or in an isolated circumstance. (e) How do the results affirm or conflict with Scripture? The interpretation process needs to coincide with principles of Scripture. To what

---

[242] Spradley, *Ethnographic Interview*, 8.

extent do the data and their interpretation correspond with the principles of Scripture and its perspective? Is the spiritual profile in harmony with the scriptural view of the spiritual dimension? And what is the relationship between the themes and Scripture.

Drawing Conclusions

After the data have been satisfactorily analyzed and interpreted, conclusions need to be drawn. They need to focus on two questions. What are the cultural themes? How do they relate to the gospel? The conclusions should point out the nature of the relationship and, in cases where the themes are in conflict with the gospel profile, the nature of the theme-related stronghold.

Sharing the Results

It is important that the conclusions are focused, clear, and practical. They should function as the stepping-stone to ministry. Two important aspects should be considered. First, the findings should be presented in a clear, direct, and easily understood manner. Second, the results should not only present the facts, but also should serve to motivate the listeners to act on the findings. The profile of the society's themes should serve to open the eyes to those natural and spiritual elements that are opposing the gospel. The better the findings are presented the more effective the ministry phase will be.

Conclusion

Spiritual diagnosis is the means by which the themes, the influencing forces, and the related strongholds can be studied and profiled. Like spiritual mapping, it has combined various research methods and made use of a variety of different resources. It differs with the mapping model in that its focus is the theme strongholds, not the demonic powers. This research model is an attempt to apply the basic principles of the current spiritual mapping concept for researching social and cultural structures.

Once the research phase is completed and the theme stronghold is profiled, a strategy needs to be set up to engage the powers, transform the themes, and break the theme stronghold. The next chapter will discuss the transformational encounter model as a means for breaking the stronghold and returning the themes to their original expression.

Chapter V
Overcoming the Demonic Cultural-Theme Stronghold through Transformational Encounters

Introduction

Once the spiritual diagnosis has been completed, the distorted and original cultural themes identified and the theme-related strongholds profiled, the next step is to create a strategy for transforming the distorted cultural themes and overcoming the demonic stronghold. The purpose of the strategy is to restore the original content, expression, understanding, and use of the cultural theme in order to establish a natural God-given pathway for introducing and establishing the gospel within the targeted group.

There are various models for changing cultures' deep-level assumptions, as well as models for dealing with the presence and influence of demonic powers. The student suggests the transformational encounter model, which deals with both the themes as well as the associated demonic powers. The model assumes that in order to restore the themes and break the related stronghold, both the natural and supernatural powers need to be encountered and overcome. The model proposes that the distorted cultural themes should be restored to their original state through initiating a deep-level cultural transformation process. This transformation is brought about through strategically planned and timed power, truth and allegiance encounters.

Before dealing with the various features of the model, the chapter will begin by analyzing and evaluating various approaches which deal with distorted cultural themes, as well as approaches for dealing with the demonic powers. This will lay the foundation for setting up the transformational encounter model. The discussion of the model will address the key features of the transformation process and show how truth, power, and allegiance encounters are the key ingredients in the process. The model will be illustrated by analyzing Jesus' approach for dealing with the distortions of the dominant Jewish theme of the Mosaic Law.

An Analysis of Existing Approaches for Transforming Cultural Themes

Cultural themes lie at the heart of culture and are integrally related to all other subsystems, structures, and parts of culture. Any changes to the themes or other worldview components will have a sweeping affect on the culture. Too many changes or too great of change will break the cohesiveness of culture, demoralize the people, and in some cases, destroy the existence of the group. Missionary anthropologists have worked on creating transformational approaches, which change cultural themes and other worldview components without breaking the group's cohesion.

Replacing Transformation

Transformation occurs through replacing the old themes with new themes. This is the traditional mission approach. The old, distorted themes are replaced with dynamic, equivalent, biblically based themes through some form of power, truth, or allegiance encounter. The new themes fulfill the same function as those themes they replaced. The success of this approach depends on the change agent's ability to contextualize the new theme. Unless the themes are integrated into the fabric of the group's worldview, the old distorted themes will resurface at a later time. Often the distorted themes have become so far removed from their intended God-given expression that replacing is the only possible approach.

Planting Transformation

A second approach, advocated by Charles Kraft, proposes planting new cultural themes as seeds, which grow and develop naturally within the culture.[243] This approach enables the themes to become naturally integrated into the culture. They are more likely to be viewed as an indigenous element. The weakness of this approach is the time it takes for the themes to become established and fully functional. Sometimes the themes are not fully realized until the second or third generation. This approach is best when the distortions are minor and do not directly conflict with the basic teachings of the gospel.

Retaining Transformation

Transformation retains the themes' forms and structures, but redefines their content. In an attempt to make the new themes acceptable to the group's culture, the third approach suggests that symbols, forms, and structures, which relate to the themes' expressions, should be retained; yet their content should be based on biblical principles. J. H. Bavinck advocates this view of transformation in his 'possessio' concept.[244] More often than not, the people's cognitive and emotional allegiance to the themes is not only tied to the themes'

---

[243] For Kraft's planting approach, see *Anthropology*, 440-41.

[244] Bavinck, 170-78.

content but to the associated expressions and forms. This approach allows people to change within the context of that which is familiar. Even though this approach takes the existing themes, their forms, and their functions seriously, it is susceptible to syncretism. This approach advocates change on the deep level, yet it is hard for most people to differentiate between form and content. In cultures, there are themes and ideas that are so integrally associated with the forms and structures that they cannot be divorced from one another, thus making 'possessio' impossible. This approach works best when the emotional ties between the theme and the forms are at a minimum.

Restoring Transformation

Transformation restores the themes to their original state. The restoration approach affirms the validity of the theme and its God-given purpose and assumes that the biblical principles are already inherent in the original content of the theme. As a result, this approach seeks to modify and restore the distorted theme to its original and intended content, expression, function, and use.

In contrast to the previous approaches, the restoration approach does not try to change, replace, or redefine the distorted theme, but strives to restore the true content, function, and expression of the theme. This approach does not require the people to break from their well-established worldview, nor does it require them to turn to culturally foreign themes and patterns, but it revitalizes the old and familiar. The restored theme creates a natural path of established cultural structures and thinking patterns through which the gospel can be presented and contextualized in a group without destroying the cohesion in the group. The people's allegiance to the themes is not challenged. The transformation process is viewed as fulfilling the purpose of the themes, rather than challenging or replacing it. It needs to be noted that there are situations where the themes are so deeply distorted that there is no longer any resemblance to the original themes. In this case, restoring the themes is equal to replacement or redefinition.

Jesus' ministry was shaped by a restoration approach as he dealt with the Jewish law. He affirmed the validity of the law and used it as a vehicle for his message. He presented himself as the one who came to fulfill the law. His purpose was to reestablish the true meaning and understanding of the law, as well as to use it to present God's redemption message. Much of his ministry (confrontation with the Pharisees and Sadducees, healing ministry, exorcisms) and teaching (Sermon on the Mount) can be interpreted in terms of Jesus' attempt to restore the Jewish theme in preparation for the salvation message.

This student acknowledges the need and use of all four approaches in dealing with a culture's worldview. The study contends, however, that the restoration approach is the most useful and applicable for dealing with cultural themes. It builds on their God-intended purpose and encourages the people to change within the confines of their culture, without needing to incorporate foreign elements. The transformational-encounter model presented below follows a restoration approach.

An Analysis of Existing Approaches for Dealing with the Demonic Powers in Structures

Just as there are many different views on the nature of the demonic influence on structures, there is a broad spectrum of approaches for responding to the powers. The study will analyze and evaluate the approaches of Walter Wink, Johann Howard Yoder, Michael Green, and C. Peter Wagner. These five models are representative of the spectrum of existing approaches.

Walter Wink's 'Sociopolitical Action' Model

In his power's trilogy, Wink suggests a model, which redeems the powers through social and political nonviolent confrontation. Wink views the powers as "part of the redemptive plan of God." He works under the assumption that "the Powers are good, the Powers are fallen, but the Powers will be redeemed."[245] Thus the goal of engaging the powers is to redeem the powers and return them to their God-given vocation and personality. Based on Eph. 3:10, the church is viewed as the primary agent for restoring the powers.

The basic formula for restoration, according to Wink, is to "acknowledge their existence, love them as creatures of God, unmask their idolatries, and stir up in them their heavenly vocation."[246] The key to discovering their vocation is through the group's repentance of their selfish pursuit of their own interests. In order to restore the vocation, the idolatry associated with the demonic powers need to be unmasked. "When a particular Power becomes idolatrous ...then that Power becomes demonic. The church's task is to unmask this idolatry and recall the Powers to their created purpose in the world."[247]

Wink proposes Jesus' third-way approach as the main tool for unmasking the powers. The approach is based on Jesus' call not to "mirror evil," but love your enemies. In contrast to the familiar ways of either fighting the powers or fleeing them, he proposes resisting the powers in a militant, nonviolent fashion while exposing their evil through responding in love to the powers. The re-

---

[245] Wink, *Engaging the Enemy*, 85.

[246] Wink, *Unmasking the Powers*, 88.

[247] Wink, *Naming the Powers*, 5.

sponse includes loving your enemy, nonviolent activism, respecting the law, overcoming the inner evil first, and taking the way of the cross. Christians are called not to simply stand against the powers, but to resist the powers with action, confrontation, and creative engagement.

Wink points out that in order to restore the powers and their structures, both the outer essence and inner spirituality need to be addressed. He emphasizes the importance of intercessory prayer for dealing with the spiritual element. He states "history belongs to the intercessor."[248] In prayer the Christian moves the hand of God by realizing his or her insufficiency in dealing with the power and calls on God to deal with and transform the powers.

Johann Howard Yoder's 'Contrast Society' Model

Yoder, in his book *The Politics of Jesus*, agrees with Wink in his overall goal of restoring the powers to their intended purpose, yet he differs with Wink in his methodology. He emphasizes the contrast between the gospel-controlled society and those controlled by the powers. The gospel represents the means for living in freedom from the powers, rather than the means to engage the powers.

There are two key features in his approach. (1) The church is God's instrument for dealing with the powers. The church models a contrasting, qualitatively different life within the midst of society. The church proclaims and demonstrates "in her life a fellowship" with Christ's victory over the powers. "...The primary social structure through which the gospel works to change other structures is that of the Christian community."[249]

(2) The primary way of dealing with the powers is exemplified by Jesus' life and his path to the cross. Jesus engaged the powers by creating a contrasting society in the midst of the old demonic structures. The new society was based on love and subordination and stood in contrast to the old ways. It was characterized by servanthood, forgiveness, and nonviolence.

The powers are confronted through the creation of such a contrast society. Through subordination and nonviolent resistance, the powers are exposed when the two societies clash. In many cases, the path will end in suffering and death as it did with Jesus on the cross. In his death on the cross, however, the powers were disarmed, made a public example of, and triumphed over by Christ (Col. 2:15).

---

[248] Wink, *Engaging the Enemy*, 298.
[249] Yoder, 157.

Both Wink and Yoder approach the issue within the context of social ethics. In contrast, Wagner, and Green respond to the powers within the context of missions.

Michael Green's 'Interdependent' Model

Michael Green in his work *Exposing the Prince of Darkness* suggests an interdependent approach that integrates and balances the spiritual and natural dimension in his response to the powers. The powers are engaged within the context of the structures they are controlling. They are addressed in the natural realm through social action and evangelism and simultaneously through prayer on a spiritual plane.

The goal of Green's approach is to overcome the influence of the powers and to restore the structures to their rightful expression. The demonic powers will eventually be destroyed.

The church is the key change agent. Green indicates, "the early Christians were a threat to Satan because they were always reaching out in service and evangelism making Christ known in the very strongholds of the Enemy."[250] The church does not preach directly to the powers, but it demonstrates God's wisdom and sovereignty to the powers through its existence as well as through preaching the gospel to the world.

The church overcomes the powers through both spiritual and social activism. He lists six tasks for engaging the powers.[251] (1) The Christians are to be watchful. (2) They are to confront the powers in prayer. Green encourages intercession as well as confessional prayer. (3) Christians and the church are called to be bold in speaking out against society's ills and deceptions by calling for repentance. (4) At times, the church will be called to resist the pressures of the powers and their earthly structures. Often the resistance will include suffering and may lead to death. In many cases the powers are overcome through martyrdom. (5) Christians are not only called to expose and speak out against the powers, but are also called to get involved in removing the demonic powers from their position of influence. This includes primarily social and political action and evangelism. (6) The engagement process should be driven by two overriding questions: What does humanity demand? What does the Bible say?

---

[250] Green, 251f.
[251] Ibid., 237-47.

C. Peter Wagner's 'Third Wave' Model

Wagner, in his books *Warfare Prayer* and *Confronting the Powers*, presents the most aggressive model for dealing with the powers. He assumes that success in evangelism depends on dealing directly with the powers. The goal is to overcome the higher powers (territorial spirits) by limiting their influence or casting them out of their territory in order to reach people with the gospel. Restoring the structures and institutions is a secondary concern.

The key to spiritual warfare is binding the strongman (Matt. 12:29). Just as Jesus bound Satan and the powers, so his disciples have been given the authority to do likewise. This includes binding territorial spirits. Wagner defines binding as "restricting the powers of evil on all levels."[252] In order to bind the powers, they need to be identified and named.

Wagner calls for seeking out the powers and directly confronting them. A number of Third Wave advocates, such as Thomas White, Clinton Arnold, and John Wimber, disagree with him on this point. They advocate an indirect approach. Arnold suggests that

> Christians do not need to feel a responsibility or a call to engage in a direct confrontation with the principalities and powers over a city, region, or a country. We appeal directly to God, who will direct his angels to fight the battles against the high-ranking powers.[253]

This confrontation may or may not occur within the context of the power's earthly manifestation.

The primary weapon of warfare is prayer, which is based on faith, obedience, and personal holiness. Related tools include using the name of Jesus, referring to the blood of Jesus, agreement in prayer, fasting, praise, and using both God's *rhema* and *logos*.[254]

An Evaluation

The models show the broad spectrum of views concerning the proper response to the demonic powers. There are five areas in which these views vary.

---

[252] Wagner, *Warfare Prayer*, 14f.

[253] Arnold, *3 Crucial Questions*, 198.

[254] Wagner differentiates between *logos*, the written word of God, and *rhema*, the spoken word of God. He suggests that both scripture and God's contemporary revelation are important tools in defeating the powers. This understanding of the word of God has revolutionized the Third Wave approach to spiritual warfare. Wagner, *Confronting the Powers*, 52-55.

(1) They differ in their understanding of the powers. Wink and Yoder equate the powers with the structures. As a result, their response focuses on the earthly structures, and their goal is to redeem the powers. Green and Wagner associate the powers with the structures. Wagner focuses on the spiritual dimension of the powers. Green tries to find a balance between dealing with the natural and supernatural dimension of the powers. Wagner and Green do not believe that the demonic powers should be saved.

(2) The nature of their response differs. Wink and Wagner call for an active response to the powers. The powers need to be sought out and engaged. The Christian needs to take the initiative. Yoder and Green take a more passive position. The powers should be engaged as they interfere in evangelism or social ethics. Once confronted, the response turns to activism.

(3) The views differ according to the type of responses. Based on three biblical terms, the responses range from resistance, to overcoming, to casting out. Resistance represents the defensive approach. All five models include resistance as the first step in responding to the powers. Yoder emphasizes active resistance. Overcoming indicates a more offensive, aggressive approach. Wink and Green seek to confront actively the powers in order to curtail their influence and control. Finally, Wagner advocates the most aggressive approach, which calls for casting out the powers. Green does not believe that there is a biblical mandate to cast out the powers. They are to be overcome and their power exposed and limited, but not cast out. In contrast, Wagner, Arnold, and many other Third-Wave advocates differentiate between ground-level exorcism, which they affirm, and strategic-level exorcism, which they reject because of a lack of a biblical mandate.

(4) The five models emphasize different tools of engagement. Wink, Yoder, and Green emphasize the use of nonviolent confrontation. Wink and Green focus on nonviolent sociopolitical activity, Yoder on a nonviolent contrast society. All three agree on the importance of prayer. Green, however, places a higher emphasis on tools such as personal holiness and evangelism than Wink or Yoder. Wagner primarily focuses on the spiritual dimension of the battle within the context of evangelism. His primary tools include personal holiness, Christ's name and blood, intercessory prayer, confessional prayer, repentance, and proclamation.

(5) There is a different understanding of the church's role. All agree that the church is the primary change agent and that the church proclaims a message to the powers through its existence. Yoder's model champions the idea that the church represents a contrasting society to the demonized society. Wink believes that the church is to proclaim a separate message of salvation to the powers. Green and Wagner believe that the church demonstrates God's wisdom to the powers by proclaiming the gospel to the nations.

Based on this analysis, the study assumes that both the natural and supernatural dimensions of the powers need to be addressed. The demonized people and structures are to be saved, but not the powers. They should be engaged in the context of doing evangelism and in bringing about sociopolitical change. The demonic powers need to be resisted and overcome. They are to be cast out of individuals when the powers have taken possession of cultural gatekeepers, but they should not be cast out of structures or territories. The church serves as the primary change agent. It demonstrates God's wisdom to the powers through its existence, its subordination to Christ, and its mission to the world. The primary tools of strategic-level spiritual warfare are personal holiness, the establishment of a contrast society, evangelism, social action, intercession, and confessional and prayer of repentance.

The Transformational-Encounter Model

The study proposes overcoming the theme strongholds through strategically planned encounters with cultural gatekeepers and the demonic powers, which transform the distorted cultural themes to their intended content, expression, use, and understanding. The aim is to restore the cultural themes so that they will serve in their intended function as a vehicle for the divine-human interaction. The following discussion will begin by looking at the nature and place of encounters in the transformation process, followed by a discussion of the overall change process.

Encounters and Transformation

Cultural theme changes are usually the result of truth, power, or allegiance encounters. They are confrontations with natural and supernatural forces who are associated with and control the themes. The aim of these encounters is to break the hold of the theme strong-holds, which keep people and their society captive. Through these encounters, the person and society's loyalties to the distorted themes are challenged and redirected to the restored, gospel-oriented themes. As a result of successful encounters, the demonic distortion is exposed, the powers' influence diminished, and their base of operation, the distorted cultural themes, destroyed.

Levels of Encounter

The encounters take place on different levels between God's forces and those of Satan. Encounters can occur between angels and the demonic powers; the church and demonic institutions; God's people and people rebelling against God; and humanity's old and new self. These encounters usually take place between like entities. However, sometimes there are crossover encounters (e.g., God's people versus demonic powers). The power and authority for these encounters are founded in God's sovereignty and Jesus' lordship and victory on the cross. It is not an encounter of equals, but encounters where the final outcome has already been determined.

The encounters are initiated in one of three ways. (1) The encounters are directly planned and set up. The circumstances are manipulated in order to create an encounter. Usually these encounters are outside of God's will and timing, thus failing and often causing great damage. (2) The encounters are indirectly planted. The seed for encounter is planted as a result of living in contrast to the established ways. As the new and the old clash, encounters evolve naturally. Jesus used this model. He never sought out encounters, but through his lifestyle and teaching, the encounters developed naturally. (3) The encounters are unplanned and appear unexpectedly. In many cases the encounters are neither expected nor planned thus catching the participating parties unprepared. As a result, the change agents miss the opportunity to challenge the demonic powers and precipitate the change process. The study suggests that the seed for encounters should be planted through living a contrasting lifestyle and engaging in them as they emerge naturally.

Types of Encounters

There are three major types of encounters: truth, power, and allegiance encounters. It is important to engage in all three of these as well as to keep them in balance.[255]

(1) Truth encounters are the confrontation between God's truth and distorted patterns of thought. The concern of this encounter is understanding. The goal is to relate scriptural principles to ideological structures of culture, show how they better meet the needs of the individual and his and her society, and integrate them into the existing worldview. Truth encounters provide the basis for the other two encounters and usually proceeds or occurs in conjunction with power encounters.

(2) The term power encounter was coined by Alan Tippett and refers to the practical demonstration that the new is better than the old and that Jesus Christ and God's Kingdom is more powerful than Satan's Kingdom and his forces.[256]

---

[255] The following discussion is based on Kraft's discussion of encounters. See Charles H. Kraft, "What Kind of Encounters Do We Need?," in *Evangelical Missions Quarterly* 27 (July 1991): 258-65.

[256] Alan R. Tippett, *Verdict Theology in Missionary Theory* (South Pasadena, CA: William Carey Library, 1973), 88-91.

The aim of the encounter is to release individuals and societies who are blinded from God's truth and cognitively and emotionally tied to distorted truths.

Tippett and most Third-Wave Spiritual Warfare advocates perceive a power encounter as a test of strength (Exodus 7-12; 1 Kings 18). Hiebert differs with this view and points out that power encounters are more often confrontations, which expose the idolatry and illegitimacy of the enemy rather than a show of strength. Through the encounters, the enemies' deception is exposed and their power, influence, and control are broken. Power encounters usually occur in the context of nonviolent resistance, subordination, suffering, and death. Jesus' power encounter on the cross was not a battle of strength, but in weakness and subordination to God unto death, he exposed and defeated the idolatry and deception of the powers. When confronting the powers associated with cultural themes, the focus should be on exposing the powers' distortion and idolatry.

(3) Truth and power encounters set up allegiance encounters. An awareness of God's truth, a demonstration of his power, and the exposing of the demonic powers provide the basis for people to change their allegiances. The goal of allegiance encounter is to bring people and creation into a right relationship with God and with one another.

There are major and minor allegiance changes. Changing allegiances on a worldview level creates a paradigm shift. The individuals change their basic outlook on life, which reorders their priorities, perceptions, relationships, and thinking and behavior patterns. This will precipitate minor allegiance encounters in which the themes are affirmed and implemented in the various life situations. When the themes are not fully integrated into all areas of life, it leads to a dual allegiance and syncretism. The more areas that have been adjusted to the new themes, the more the demonic control diminishes. The goal of a theme-allegiance change is to bring about an allegiance encounter concerning the people's relationship with Christ.

Jesus' ministry was characterized by all three encounters. He consistently proclaimed the truth by challenging the people to a new understanding of their relationship with God and the law. He engaged in power encounters with the Pharisees and the demonic powers. He called on the people to change their allegiance from a sinful path to an undivided commitment to God. Jesus consistently challenged the current understanding and practice of the law. He broke the traditional boundaries set by the Pharisees. He challenged the established understanding of the law by living out and teaching a reformed understanding of the law. He cast out the demons and demonstrated God's power. He preached the coming of the new kingdom and proclaimed a new ethic (e.g., Sermon on the Mount). His death and resurrection was the climax of all the previous encounters. It was the key encounter, which defeated the powers and established the new paradigm for relating to God.[257]

Warfare Prayer as a Means for Encounters

The demonic powers associated with the themes are confronted through warfare prayer. Through intercession and confession, Christians take an active part in the battle between God's forces and those of Satan. Wagner points out that the purpose of prayer is "not to persuade or influence God, but to join forces with him against the enemy."[258]

Two types of prayers are used in confronting the powers. (1) Intercessory prayer intercedes for individuals, their society, and the society's gatekeepers. Through prayer, the powers are engaged and their influence curtailed. In prayer God is petitioned to come against, overcome, and expose the powers.

(2) Confessional prayer includes both worship and repentance. The powers are confronted through confessing and proclaiming Christ's victory and lordship over the powers in praise and worship.

Through the confession of sin, the powers' stronghold is broken. Through repentance the powers' distortion is exposed and their base of influence eliminated. This includes both individual and corporate repentance.[259] Through intercession and confession, the demonic powers are addressed and confronted, assuring the success of the change process.

Truth, power, and allegiance encounters are the primary tool in securing the transformation of the themes. Both the human powers and demonic powers are confronted through these encounters. As the truth is revealed, God's power is demonstrated and the powers and their distortions exposed. As a result, people will be able to transfer their allegiance to the new theme. What place the encounters play in the overall scheme of the transformation process will be discussed below.

The Transformation Process

The aim of the transformation process is to replace the society's existing and distorted themes with the original theme in order to create a better society and

---

[257] Hiebert and Shaw, 174, present a list of Jesus' encounters which are mentioned in John's gospel.

[258] Wagner, *Warfare Prayer*, 106.

[259] For discussions on identificational repentance, see Wagner, *Warfare Prayer*, 125-32; John Dawson, *Healing America's Wounds* (Ventura, CA: Regal Books, 1994); and Arnold, *3 Crucial Questions*, 177-85.

reduce the resistance toward the gospel. Wallace calls this type of transformation a "Revitalization Movement" and defines it as "a deliberate, organized, conscious effort by members of a society to construct a more satisfying culture."[260] The following discussion of the transformation process is based on Wallace's revitalization model. The process will be illustrated by Jesus' confrontation with the Pharisees and their distorted understanding of the law.[261]

The Steady State

Before the transformation process begins, the distorted themes are firmly established in the society and serve as a key assumption that uphold the culture's cohesiveness. The themes are fulfilling their functions and the people do not perceive a need for changing or modifying the themes. The demonic powers have created a theme-based network of beliefs, values, customs, rituals, and other structures, which create resistance among the people to the gospel. At this stage the missionary or change advocate should enter the culture, become established, study the culture (spiritual diagnosis), identify with the people and their customs, begin interceding for the group, identify the original themes and integrate them into his or her life, and model it in his or her relationship with the people. During this time, the foundation for a successful change process is laid.

Jesus identified with the culture. He grew up and lived in it, learned its ways, studied the law, and took ownership of the original intention and understanding of the law. This phase took thirty years of his life and was established in the Jewish culture. This gave him the right to speak out against the distorted view of the law and the demonic forces behind it.

Period of Increased Stress and Cultural Distortion

The cultural cohesion of a society becomes threatened when events (e.g., catastrophes, military defeat, epidemics, etc.), innovations, increased oppression, or outside influences challenge the validity of the existing themes and question

---

[260] Anthony F. C. Wallace, "Revitalization Movements," *American Anthropologist* 58 (March 1956): 265.

[261] Kraft describes Jesus' relationship to the Jewish culture as follows: "Jesus is our model here, as in all other matters. He lived within the cultural structuring around Him and according to most of the worldview assumptions underlying that culture. There were, to be sure, differences in some of the things He assumed, differences that came from His Kingdom perspective ... But the main thing that differed about Jesus was His commitment to live within those structures in total faithfulness to God. He did not introduce new structures; He used the old structures differently than did the society (the world) around Him." Kraft, 359.

their legitimacy. The themes fail to meet the needs created by the new situation. As a result, the stress level for individuals increases. If the stress level remains high for a long period and affects a majority of the society's people, cultural distortion occurs and the culture begins to deteriorate. Many begin to look for alternative solutions to their problems, which create an openness to change or modify the old themes.

During this time, the demonic powers will seek to maintain their power base by shifting their influence from one theme to another or introducing new distorted themes. The change advocate needs to be aware of the growing stress level and find ways to build on the growing disillusionment. He or she needs to reach out to those who are oppressed, dissatisfied, and disillusioned because of the existing themes. Through truth encounters and demonstrating the themes, the advocate will be able to lead some of these individuals to convert to the new themes. As more and more people overcome the stress through turning to the new themes, a revitalization movement is able to emerge.

In *The Deep-Sea Canoe*, Alan Tippett presents the natural progression of how people convert to new ideas such as the gospel or a new theme.[262]

The individual first becomes aware of the need for change and is confronted with the prospects of the restored cultural theme. The positives and negatives of change are considered during a decision-making phase. During this time, the demonic powers are actively working to influence the individual so that he or she will retain his or her allegiance to the old theme or to an alternate distorted theme.

At some point the individual is forced to make a decision for or against the new theme. Tippett refers to this event as a power encounter which leads to an allegiance encounter. Through the power encounter, the old theme is rejected and the new theme is embraced and the demonic stronghold is broken and the influence of the demonic powers is overcome. Once the new theme is accepted, it is incorporated into the matrix of the individual's life. He or she will continue to face various minor allegiance encounters as the new theme challenges the old, deep-seated thinking and behavior patterns which have been created by the distorted theme. As the process matures, the individual becomes an advocate of change and helps others to turn to the new theme.

At the beginning stages, the outside advocate will function as the primary change agent. For the change process to affect the society as a whole, however, the implementation process needs to shift from the outsider advocate to an

---

[262] Alan R. Tippett, *The Deep Sea Canoe* (South Pasadena, CA: William Carey Library, 1977), 42.

insider advocate. Kraft illustrates the progression of this shift as follows:[263] Through the ministry of the outsider advocate, a cultural insider accepts the new theme and implements it into his or her life. As it changes, he or she becomes an implementer and insider advocate who is able to reach others within the group.

Throughout the process, it is important to reach out to the various existing and potential gatekeepers. In order to change the society, the gatekeepers need to be won for the cause. Incorporating a new idea on societal level must work with and through the local gatekeepers. The demonic powers have an invested interest in the gatekeepers and will seek to keep them tied to the old themes. In many cases, the conversion process with gatekeepers will require a significant power encounter.

Jesus tapped into the cultural distortion of the first-century Jewish society. The Roman occupation and the oppression by the religious leaders and their understanding and implementation of the Mosaic Law created an oppressed group of people who were seeking change. Jesus reached out to these people and their potential gatekeepers and discipled them in the new understanding of the law. Through the discipling process, this group became the advocates and implementers of the restored theme.

Period of Revitalization

As more and more people accept and become implementers of the new theme, a movement develops which seeks to restore the cultural cohesion by creating a society-wide paradigm shift centered on the new theme. As the movement grows and becomes a formidable force, it will come into conflict with the old themes and the related power structures. The tension between the old and the new increases and leads to one major or a series of smaller power encounters. If successful, the existing theme strongholds are broken and the related powers are unmasked and their power diminished.

Emergence of a Leader

As the movement develops, a leader of the movement will emerge. In order to bring about the change he or she will need to be an insider, have a culturally legitimate claim to authority; be respected; have a good understanding of the dynamics of a change process; have a vision for the people; be able to visualize the needed changes; be committed to the new themes; and live and operate within the confines of the culturally acceptable ways, yet willing to experiment and go beyond the socially permissible range of variability. In many

---

[263] Kraft, *Anthropology*, 409.

cases, the leader will emerge from within the group and grow into leadership, rather than join from the outside as an established leader.

The Theme Is Communicated

As the movement grows, the message of the theme is communicated to the society through truth encounters. The new theme should be verbally communicated, modeled, and demonstrated. The communication should be receptor oriented; clear, simple, and observable; include formal and informal channels of communication; follow along culturally accepted patterns of communication; and show how the new theme can meet the needs and challenges created by the new situation. The goal of the communication is twofold. It is to persuade people to adapt the new theme into their life and should expose the distorted themes and the powers, which lie behind them.

The new themes need to relate to everyday life situations. Jesus communicated his understanding of the law through two simple and clear sayings: "love God with all your heart" and "love your neighbor as yourself." He demonstrated these sayings and related them to everyday situations through parables. As a result of Jesus' communication, the people were able to make a clear distinction between the old and the new.[264]

A Contrast Society Is Created

As the new theme becomes integrated into the lives of the people, a contrast society will form. It should break with the old; yet maintain continuity with the familiar. If the changes are too radical or too fast, the continuity and cohesiveness of the culture is broken and the majority of the people will reject the movement. The leaders of the movement will need to be aware of those radical forces , which want to accelerate the change process by bringing about too many changes too fast.

In conjunction with the creation of the contrast society, it is important that the people begin to deal with their history. They need to become aware of corporate and individual sins, which have created the cultural distortion, acknowledge the past and present sins, identify with them, and repent of them. At this stage, it is possible to begin introducing the gospel to those who have embraced the new theme. The individual as well as societal identification and repentance are major parts of the change process.

Once the movement threatens the existing power structures, the opposition to the new movement increases and attempts to suppress the movement begin. The attacks take place on both the natural, as well as the supernatural level.

---

[264] Kraft discusses the nature of Jesus' communication in Kraft, *Anthropology*, 443-44.

Truth and power encounters become more frequent, leading up to a major confrontation. As Jesus' influence grew, the opposition to the existing powers grew stronger. Through various smaller power and truth encounters, the tension with the Pharisees and the demonic powers grew, leading to a major confrontation on the cross.

The Key Power Encounter

Once the tension has reached a breaking point, there will be a power encounter between the old and new, between the gatekeepers holding on to the old themes, and representatives of the restored themes, as well as between God's forces and the demonic powers. This confrontation will occur either as one major encounter or through a series of smaller, yet significant, encounters. The encounter will center on the key gatekeepers associated with the old themes. Through direct or indirect confrontation, their authority and power is challenged. At the same time, the demonic powers are encountered through prayer. Both areas of confrontation are important in order to engage all the forces involved with the themes. It is crucial to wait on God's timing. Many encounters end in apparent defeat due to being premature. The power encounters need to evolve naturally and should not be manufactured.

The confrontation can take on various forms. It may be a one-on-one challenge, a challenge between two groups of people, a stand off, a truth declaration, a violent confrontation, a strike, a public recanting of past sins, etc. Each cultural situation is unique. Each stronghold associated with the theme will be different and will require a unique strategy of engagement. The nature and content of the theme, the power structure of the society, the gatekeeper, and the development of the contrast society will also shape the nature of the encounter.

Jesus confronted the powers on the cross. In this confrontation, the distortion of the law was exposed, the idolatry of the earthly powers unmasked, the demonic powers overcome and defeated, and the related stronghold broken. In his death and resurrection, the new understanding and use of the theme became established.

Result of the Power Encounter

Spiritual warfare advocates differ as to the results of these power encounters. The commonly held view follows the following scheme. The local traditions, gatekeepers, spiritual powers, etc. are confronted so that God's power is revealed and established. As a result, people's eyes are opened to the new theme or the gospel, which leads to receptivity and large-scale conversion. Hiebert points out that scripture portrays a different view of the results of power and truth encounters. The encounters lead to an initial positive response by the people, but are then followed by increased persecution and the rise of different strongholds. Hiebert notes that the history of such power encounters is such that, after the preliminary confrontation, the powers mobilize in opposition.[265]

This scheme is consistent in the ministry of Jesus and the apostles. This fact does not negate the value of power encounters, but shows that the fruitful ground gained in power encounters is limited and requires immediate harvesting.

Reorganization

It is important to react quickly to the new situation by integrating the new themes, and establishing continuity, a sense of security, and a cultural balance. The power encounter creates a vacuum. It tears down old established thought patterns and worldview paradigms and creates a feeling of insecurity and discontinuity. The faster and more in-depth this can be done the more chances there is that the theme will become established on a group-wide basis.

New State of Being

The new themes will create opportunities for more changes. At this point, the gospel can and should be introduced on a societal level. It should be contextualized and introduced in conjunction with the new theme. The power encounter will provide a window of opportunity for the theme as well as the gospel. Once the foundation of the old stronghold has been broken, it is important to tear down all parts of the stronghold so as not to allow a remnant to become the source of a new stronghold. In many cases the demonic powers will either shift their emphasis to other themes or areas, which they control, or they will establish one or more alternative themes that will challenge the new themes as the appropriate alternative to the old ones. Another area to which the demonic turn is factionalism. It usually rises shortly after the major power encounters. As soon as the demonic powers find a new avenue to exert their control and oppression and persecution are reappear.

The Change Process and the Gospel

What role does the gospel play in the transformation process? Its role is dependent on the nature of the cultural theme and the society's level of resistance to the gospel. (1) In some cases the transformation of the themes is part of the overall message of the gospel. The themes change as the society accepts the gospel. This is possible when there is a general openness to the

---

[265] Hiebert, "Spiritual Warfare," 238.

gospel. The restored themes are a product of the gospel. (2) The gospel is part of the transformation process of the themes. The gospel message is part of the expression and content of the original themes. This is possible wherever the Christian faith is part of the cultural matrix of the society, but not it's driving force (e.g., post-Christian Europe). The themes serve as the vehicle for introducing or establishing the gospel. (3) Finally, the gospel is responsible for the change process of the themes, but is not introduced until the new themes have been established. This is the model that needs to be used in societies that are strongly resistant or actively opposed to the culture. The new theme functions as the gate through which the gospel is introduced.

Conclusion

The transformational-encounter model suggests that the original themes are restored through a series of encounters, which begin on an individual level and then move to a societal level. As the old and the new clash, the existing natural and supernatural powers and their theme-based power structures are challenged. As the themes' distortion and the powers' idolatry is unmasked and the theme strongholds broken, the new theme is integrated into the fabric of the society's worldview. This reduces the resistance to the gospel and creates a window of opportunity for introducing and contextualizing the gospel into the society.

Chapter VI
Conclusion

Missionary anthropologists such as Charles Kraft, Paul Hiebert, and Louis Luzbetak have shown that cultural themes play an important role in missions. They either function as a helpful vehicle assisting the evangelistic efforts, or they operate as forces, which hinder the advancement of the gospel. Based on this fact, this study has proposed the thesis that cultural themes, which have been distorted by demonic powers and human sinfulness, are one of the main causes for a group's resistance to the gospel. The study suggests that through restoring the distorted theme to its original state, the demonic stronghold is broken, leading to a more favorable attitude toward the gospel and increasing the effectiveness of evangelistic missions.

The study has investigated the claims set forth by the thesis and has come to the following conclusions. (1) The original function of the cultural themes is to assist individuals and the societies in living out their relationship to God. The study points out that God has a calling and vocation for the various peoples, which are expressed and become functional through the themes. These themes are culture's built-in structures through which the gospel can be effectively introduced and contextualized.

(2) Distorted cultural themes are a major cause for a group's resistance to the gospel. The study has shown that through the cultural pull and pressure forces, the themes shape and condition the thinking and behaving patterns of the individual and his culture. Further, the study has demonstrated that through human sinfulness, demonic powers are able to associate with the themes and distort their content, expression, use, and understanding, leading to a cultural makeup, which is in conflict with the gospel.

(3) Distorted themes develop into cultural theme strongholds. Because of the natural control mechanisms associated with the cultural themes, the distortion creates a mental stronghold, which keeps the people captive on a cognitive and emotional level to a distorted view of reality and the gospel message.

(4) The theme-based resistance is broken through transformational encounters. The study has illustrated that by identifying the themes and strongholds and by transforming the distorted cultural themes to their original state through transformational encounters, the theme stronghold is broken; thus the demonic influence is curtailed and the group's perception of the gospel becomes more favorable.

What impact do these conclusions have on missions?

(1) The theme concept provides an effective vehicle for introducing and contextualizing the gospel. Once the gospel is associated with cultural themes, then the society will be more willing to accept and integrate the full gospel message into its cultural matrix. As a result, the gospel will present itself as a message of hope, which creates better culture bearers, rather than a force that threatens the cultural cohesiveness.

(2) In order to effectively proclaim the gospel to a resistant people group, it is important to first deal with the group's distorted themes and the related demonic powers. Often mission efforts are exclusively focused on the individual and fail to deal with the individual's culture and the forces associated with the culture. As a result, the demonic powers are able to enter a society undetected and exert their spiritual influence over a society through the existing cultural framework. Not until the missionary deals with the underlying cause of a person's resistance will he or she be able to effectively evangelize.

(3) The mission enterprise needs to deal with both the natural and supernatural causes for resistance. The study has demonstrated that there is a cause and effect relationship between the supernatural and natural realm, which comes into play when dealing with the cultural theme strongholds. In order to bring about change, both the natural and supernatural causes need to be considered and addressed.

(4) Power encounters are a vital part of the mission process. The study has demonstrated that the transformational encounter process brings about changes on both the natural and supernatural level. Through power encounters, demonic powers and their distortions are unmasked, and the redemptive power of the gospel is demonstrated. Power encounters create an environment where people are more willing to hear and receive the gospel.

(5) Mission groups should target resistant groups. In the last part of the twentieth century, the trend in missions has been on emphasizing those areas and peoples who are responsive to the gospel. This study suggests that mission agencies should invest significant resources to resistant people groups. They should be targeted and significant resources should be invested in identifying and overcoming their theme strongholds.

The study has presented a thesis, which deals with peoples' resistance to the gospel. It has presented a possible cause for the resistance and has proposed a strategy for breaking through the resistance. The goal of the study has been to explain the culture-theme stronghold concept and show how one can effectively deal with the distorted themes in order to increase the effectiveness of evangelistic missions.

Bibliography

Books

Arnold, Clinton E. *Ephesians: Power and Magic*. Grand Rapids: Baker Book House, 1989.

___. *Powers of Darkness: Principalities and Powers in Paul's Letters*. Downers Grove, IL: InterVarsity Press, 1992.

___. *The Colossian Syncretism: The Interface between Christianity and Folk Belief*. Grand Rapids: Baker, 1996.

___. *3 Crucial Questions about Spiritual Warfare*. Grand Rapids: Baker Book House, 1997.

Basso, Keith, and Henry A. Selby, eds. *Meaning in Anthropology*. Albuquerque, NM: University of New Mexico Press, 1976.

Bateson, Gregory. *Steps to an Ecology of Mind*. New York: Ballantine Books, 1972.

Bavinck, J. H. *An Introduction to the Science of Missions*. Translated by David Hugh Freeman. Phillipsburg, NJ: Presbyterian & Reformed Pub. Co., 1960.

Beckett, Bob. *Commitment to Conquer*. Grand Rapids: Chosen Books, 1997.

Benedict, Ruth. *The Chrysanthemum and the Sword: Patterns of Japanese Culture*. Boston: Houghton & Mifflin, 1946.

___. *Patterns of Culture*. New York: Penguin Books, 1946.

Berkhof, Hendrikus. *Christ and the Powers*. Scottsdale, PA: Herald Press, 1962.

Bierstedt, Robert. *The Social Order*. 3d ed. New York: McGraw-Hill, 1970.

Bright, John. *A History of Israel*. 3d ed. Philadelphia: Westminster Press, 1981.

Buber, Martin. *Israel and the World*. New York: Schocken Books, 1948.

Bultmann, Rudolf. *The New Testament and Mythology and Other Basic Writings*. Philadelphia: Fortress Press, 1984.

Burgess, Stanley M., and Gary B. McGee, eds. *Dictionary of Pentecostal and Charismatic Movements*. Grand Rapids: Zondervan, 1989.

Burnett, David. *Clash of Worlds*. Nashville: Oliver Nelson, 1992.

Bush, Louis. *AD 2000 and Beyond Handbook*. Colorado Springs: AD 2000 and Beyond Movement, 1993.

Carid, George B. *Principalities and the Powers: A Study in Pauline Theology*. Oxford: Clarendon Press, 1956.

Carr, Wesley. *Angels and Principalities*. Cambridge: Cambridge University Press, 1981.

Carson, D. A., ed. *Biblical Interpretation and the Church, Text and Context*. Grand Rapids: Baker Book House, 1984.

Conley, William. *The Kalimantan Kenyah*. Nutley, NJ: Presbyterian & Reformed Pub., 1973.

Conn, Harvie M. *Eternal Word and Changing Worlds: Theology, Anthropology, and Mission in Trialogue*. Phillipsburg, NJ: Presbyterian & Reformed Pub., 1984.

Davidson, Gustav. *A Dictionary of Angels, Including the Fallen Angels*. New York: Free Press, 1971.

Dawson, John. *Healing America's Wounds*. Ventura, CA: Regal Books, 1994.

___. *Taking Our City for God*. Lake Mary, FL: Creation House, 1989.

Dayton, Edward R., and David A. Fraser. *Planning Strategies for World Evangelization*. Grand Rapids: Wm. B. Eerdmans Pub., 1980.

de Toqueville, Alexis. *Democracy in America*. 2 vols. New York: Alfred A. Knopf, 1945.

Dickason, C. Fred. *Demon Possession and the Christian*. Chicago: Moody Press, 1987.

Dibelius, Martin. *Die Geisterwelt im Glauben des Paulus*. Göttingen, Germany: Vandenhoeck & Ruprecht, 1909.

Durkheim, Emile. *The Elementary Forms of the Religious Life*. New York: Free Press, 1965.

Eliade, Mircea. *The Encyclopedia of Religion*. Vol. 4. New York: Macmillan Pub. Co., 1987.

Fischer, Hans, ed. *Ethnologie, Einführung und Überblick*. Berlin: Dietrich Reimer Verlag, 1992.

Frangipane, Francis. *The Three Battlegrounds*. Marion, IA: Advancing Church Pub., 1989.

Fritsch, Siegfried. *Der Geist über Deutschland*. Schorndorf, Germany: Johannes Fix Verlag, 1985.

Garrett, Duane A., and Richard R. Melick, Jr., eds. *Authority and Interpretation: A Baptist Perspective*. Grand Rapids: Baker Book House, 1987.

Garbarino, Merwyn S. *Sociocultural Theory in Anthropology: A Short History*. Prospect Heights, IL: Waveland Press, 1983.

Gover, Geoffrey. *The American People*. New York: Norton & Co., 1948.

Gover, Geoffrey, and J. Richman. *The People of Great Russia*. London: Cresset Press, 1949.

Green, Michael. *Exposing the Prince of Darkness*. Ann Arbor, MI: Servant Books, 1981.

Grieg, Gary S., and Kevin N. Springer. *The Kingdom and the Power*. Ventura, CA: Regal Books, 1993.

Gross, Edward N. *Miracles, Demons, and Spiritual Warfare: An Urgent Call for Discernment*. Grand Rapids: Baker Book House, 1990.

Grunlan, Stephan A., and Marvin K. Mayers. *Cultural Anthropology: A Christian Perspective*. Grand Rapids: Zondervan Pub., 1988.

Hall, Edward T. *Understanding Cultural Differences: Keys to Success in West Germany, France, and the United States*. Yarmouth, ME: Intercultural Press, 1990.

Hallowell, A. I. *Culture and Experience*. Philadelphia: University of Pennsylvania Press, 1955.

Hammond, Peter B., ed. *Cultural and Social Anthropology: Introducing Readings in Ethnology*. New York: Macmillan, 1964.

Hesselgrave, David J. *Communicating Christ Cross-Culturally*. Grand Rapids: Zondervan Pub., 1991.

___. *Today's Choices for Tomorrow's Mission: An Evangelical Perspective on Trends and Issues in Missions*. Grand Rapids: Zondervan Pub., 1988.

Hiebert, Paul G. *Anthropological Insights for Missionaries*. Grand Rapids: Baker Book House, 1985.

___. *Anthropological Reflections on Missiological Issues*. Grand Rapids: Baker Book House, 1994.

___. *Cultural Anthropology*. Grand Rapids: Baker Book House, 1983.

Hill, Richard. *We Europeans*. Brussels, Belgium: Europublications, 1992.

Jacobs, Cindy. *Possessing the Gates of the Enemy*. Grand Rapids: Chosen Books, 1991.

Kearney, Michael. *World View*. Novato, CA: Chandler & Sharp Pub., 1984.

Kinnaman, Gary D. *Overcoming the Dominion of Darkness*. Old Tappan, NJ: Chosen Books, 1990.

Kluckhohn, Clyde. *Mirror of Man*. New York: McGraw-Hill, 1949.

Kluckhohn, Florence R., and Fred L. Strodtbeck. *Variations in Value Orientations*. Evanston, IL: Row, Peterson & Co., 1961.

König, Adrio. *The Eclipse of Christ in Eschatology: Towards a Christ-Centered Approach*. Grand Rapids: William B. Eerdmans Pub., 1989.

Kopfermann, Wolfram. *Macht Ohne Auftrag*. Emmelsbüll, Germany: C und P Verlag, 1994.

Kradiner, Abram. *The Individual and His Society*. New York: Columbia University Press, 1939.

Kraft, Charles H. *Anthropology for Christian Witness*. Maryknoll, NY: Orbis Books, 1996.

__. *Christianity in Culture: A Study in Dynamic Biblical Theologizing in Cross-Cultural Perspective*. Maryknoll, NY: Orbis Books, 1979.

__. *Christianity with Power*. Ann Arbor, MI: Servant Pub., 1993.

__. *Defeating Dark Angels: Breaking Demonic Oppression in the Believer's Life*. Ann Arbor, MI: Servants Pub., 1992.

Kraft, Charles H., and Mark White, eds. *Behind Enemy Lines: An Advanced Guide to Spiritual Warfare*. Ann Arbor, MI: Vine Books, 1994.

Kraft, Marguerite G. *Worldview and the Communication of the Gospel*. South Pasadena, CA: William Carey Library, 1979.

Kroeber, Alfred L. *The Nature of Culture*. Chicago: University of Chicago Press, 1952.

Kroeber, Alfred L., and Clyde Kluckhohn. *Culture: A Critical Review of Concepts and Definitions*. Vol. 47, no. 1. Papers of the Peabody Museum of American Archaeology and Ethnology. Cambridge: Harvard University, 1952.

Ladd, George Eldon. *A Theology of the New Testament*. Grand Rapids: William B. Eerdmans Pub., 1974.

Lewis, C. S. *The Screwtape Letters*. New York: Macmillan, 1982.

Lewis, Oscar. *Life in a Mexican Village*. Urbana, IL: University of Illinois Press, 1951.

Lingenfelter, Sherwood. *Transforming Culture: A Challenge for Christian Mission*. Grand Rapids: Baker Book House, 1992.

Linthicum, Robert C. *City of God, City of Satan: A Biblical Theology of the Urban Church*. Grand Rapids: Zondervan Pub., 1991.

Luzbetak, Louis J. *The Church and Cultures: New Perspectives in Missiological Anthropology*. Maryknoll, NY: Orbis Books, 1991.

MacMullen, Ramsay. *Christianizing the Roman Empire*. New Haven, CT: Yale University Press, 1984.

Malcolm, Andrew H. *The Canadians*. New York: Time Books, 1985.

Mansfield, Stephen, ed. *Releasing Destiny: A Spiritual Warfare Manual for Nashville and Country Music*. Nashville: Daniel 1 School of Leadership, 1993.

Manson, T. W., ed. *A Companion to the Bible*. Edinburgh: T & T Clark, 1939.

Marsh, David. *The Germans*. London: Century Hutchinson, 1989.

McAlpine, Thomas H. *Facing the Powers: What Are the Options?* Monrovia, CA: MARC, 1991.

McGavran, Donald A. *Understanding Church Growth*. 2d ed. Grand Rapids: William B. Eerdmans Pub., 1980.

Mead, Margaret. *And Keep Your Powder Dry*. New York: Morrow, 1942.

___. *Coming of Age in Samoa*. New York: Morrow, 1928.

___. *Sex and Temperament in Three Primitive Societies*. New York: Morrow, 1935.

Montgomery, John Warwick. *Principalities and Powers: The World of the Occult*. Minneapolis: Bethany Fellowship, 1973.

Moreau, A. Scott. *Essentials of Spiritual Warfare, Equipped to Win the Battle*. Wheaton, IL: Harold Shaw Pub., 1997.

Mott, Stephen C. *Biblical Ethics and Social Change*. New York: Oxford University Press, 1982.

Mouw, Richard J. *Politics and the Biblical Drama*. Grand Rapids: William B. Eerdmans Pub., 1976.

Müller, Klaus W., ed. *Mission als Kampf mit den Mächten: Zum Missiologischen Konzept des "Power Encounter."* Bonn, Germany: Verlag für Kultur und Wissenschaft, 1993.

Murphy, Edward F. *The Handbook for Spiritual Warfare*. Nashville: Thomas Nelson Pub., 1992.

Newport, John P. *Life's Ultimate Questions: A Contemporary Philosophy of Religion*. Dallas, TX: Word Pub., 1989.

Nida, Eugene. *Customs and Culture*. South Pasadena, CA: William Carey Library, 1954.

Niebuhr, H. Richard. *Christ and Culture*. New York: Harper Torchbooks, 1951.

Otis, George, Jr. *The Last of the Giants*. Tarrytown, NY: Chosen Books, 1991.

___. Spiritual Mapping Field Guide: North American Edition. Lynnwood, WA: Sentinal Group, 1993.

___. *Strongholds of the 10/40 Window*. Seattle: YWAM Pub., 1995.

___. *The Twilight Labyrinth*. Grand Rapids: Chosen Books, 1997.

Page, Syndey H. T. *Powers of Evil*. Grand Rapids: Baker Book House, 1995.

Panoff, Michael, and Michel Perrin. *Taschenwörterbuch der Ethnologie*. Berlin: Dietrich Reimer Verlag, 1982.

Powlison, David. *Power Encounters*. Grand Rapids: Baker Book House, 1995.

Peck, M. Scott. *People of the Lie: The Hope for Healing Human Evil*. New York: Touchtone Books, 1983.

Peretti, Frank E. *Piercing the Darkness*. Westchester, IL: Crossway Books, 1989.

___. *This Present Darkness*. Wheaton, IL: Crossway Books, 1986.

Redfield, Robert. *Peasant Society and Culture*. Chicago: University of Chicago Press, 1956.

___. *Tepoztlan: A Mexican Village*. Chicago: University of Chicago Press, 1930.

Richardson, Don. *Eternity in Their Hearts*. Ventura, CA: Regal Books, 1985.

___. *Peace Child*. Glendale, CA: Regal Books, 1974.

Robb, John D. *Focus! The Power of People Groups Thinking*. Monrovia, CA: MARC, 1994.

Rohrbach, Hans. *Unsichtbare Mächte und die Macht Jesu*. Wuppertal, Germany: R. Brockhaus Verlag, 1985.

Rommen, Edward, ed. *Spiritual Power and Missions: Raising the Issues*. Pasadena, CA: William Carey Library, 1995.

Rupp, Gordon. Principalities and Powers: Studies in the Christian Conflict in History. Nashville: Abingdon Press, 1952.

Russell, D. S. *The Method of Jewish Apocalyptic*. Philadelphia: Westminster Press, 1964.

Russell, Jefferey Burton. *The Prince of Darkness*. Ithaca, NY: Cornell University Press, 1988.

Scherer, James A., and Stephan B. Bevans, eds. *New Directions in Mission and Evangelization I: Basic Statements 1974-1991*. Maryknoll, NY: Orbis Books, 1992.

Schlier, Henrich. *Principalities and Powers in the New Testament*. New York: Herder & Herder, 1961.

Schreiter, Robert J. *Constructing Local Theologies*. Maryknoll, NY: Orbis Books, 1985.

Shaw, Daniel R. *Kandila*. Ann Arbor, MI: University of Michigan, 1990.

___. *Transculturation*. Pasadena, CA: William Carey Press, 1988.

Silvoso, Ed. *That None Should Perish*. Ventura, CA: Regal Books, 1994.

Smalley, William A. *Readings in Missionary Anthropology II*. Pasadena, CA: William Carey Library, 1978.

Spradley, James P. *The Ethnographic Interview*. Fort Worth, TX: Harcourt Brace Jovanovich College Pub., 1979.

___. *Participant Observation*. New York: Holt, Reinhart & Winston, 1979.

Spradley, James P., and David McCurdy. *Anthropology: The Cultural Perspective*. New York: Wiley, 1975.

Swartley, Willard M., ed. *Essays on Spiritual Bondage and Deliverance*. Occasional Papers No. 11. Elkhart, IN: Institute of Mennonite Studies, 1988.

Tippett, Alan R. *The Deep Sea Canoe*. South Pasadena, CA: William Carey Library, 1977.

___. *Solomon Islands Christianity: A Study in Growth and Obstruction*. London: Lutterworth Press, 1967.

___. *Verdict Theology in Missionary Theory*. Pasadena, CA: William Carey Library, 1973.

Unger, Merrill F. *Biblical Demonology: A Study of Spiritual Forces at Work Today*. Grand Rapids: Kregel Pub., 1994.

van der Toorn, Karel, Bob Becking, and Pieter W. van der Horst, eds. *Dictionary of Deities and Demons in the Bible*. New York: E. J. Brill, 1995.

Van Rheenen, Gailyn. *Communicating Christ in Animistic Contexts*. Grand Rapids: Baker Book House, 1991.

Wagner. C. Peter. *Confronting the Powers*. Ventura, CA: Regal Books, 1996.

___. *Spreading the Fire: A New Look at Acts – God's Training Manual for Every Christian*. Ventura, CA: Regal Books, 1994.

___. *The Third Wave of the Holy Spirit*. Ann Arbor, MI: Vine Books, 1988.

___. *Warfare Prayer*. Ventura, CA: Regal Books, 1992.

___, ed. *Breaking the Strongholds in the City: How to Use Spiritual Mapping to Make Your Prayers More Strategic, Effective, and Targeted*. Ventura, CA: Regal Books, 1993.

___, ed. *Engaging the Enemy*. Ventura, CA: Regal Books, 1991.

Wagner, C. Peter, and F. Douglas Pennoyer, eds. *Wrestling with Dark Angels*. Ventura, CA: Regal Books, 1990.

Warner, Timothy M. *Spiritual Warfare*. Wheaton, IL: Crossway Books, 1991.

White, Tom. *The Believer's Guide to Spiritual Warfare*. Ann Arbor, MI: Servant Pub., 1990.

___. *Breaking Strongholds: How Spiritual Warfare Sets Captives Free*. Ann Arbor, MI: Vine Books, 1993.

William, Daniel Day. *The Demonic and the Divine*. Edited by Stacy A. Evans. Minneapolis: Fortress Press, 1990.

Williams, Thomas Rhys. *Introduction to Socialization*. St. Louis: C. V. Mosby, 1972.

Wimber, John. *Spiritual Warfare*. Anaheim, CA: Mercy Pub., 1988.

Wimber, John, and Kevin Springer. *Power Evangelism*. San Francisco: Harper & Co., 1986.

Wink, Walter. *Engaging the Powers*. Minneapolis: Fortress Press, 1992.

___. *Naming the Powers*. Philadelphia: Fortress Press, 1984.

___. *Unmasking the Powers*. Philadelphia: Fortress Press, 1986.

Winter, Ralph D., and Steven C. Hawthorne, eds. *Perspective on the World Christian Movement*. Rev. ed. Pasadena, CA: William Carey Library, 1992.

Wright, Nigel. *The Satan Syndrome: Putting the Power of Darkness in Its Place*. Grand Rapids: Zondervan Pub., 1990.

Yoder, John Howard. *The Politics of Jesus*. Grand Rapids: William B. Eerdmans Pub., 1972.

Articles

Amborn, Hermann. „Strukturalismus. Theorie und Methode." In *Ethnologie: Einführung und Überblick*, ed. Hans Fischer, 337-65. Berlin: Dietrich Reimer Verlag, 1992.

Arnold, Clinton E. "Principalities and Powers in Recent Interpretation." *Catalyst* 17 (February 1991): 4-5.

Benedict, Ruth. "Configurations of Culture in North America." *American Anthropologists* 34 (1932): 1-27.

Buber, Martin. "The Gods of the Nations and God." In *Israel and the World*. New York: Schocken Books, 1948.

Bultmann, Rudolf, ed. "New Testament and Mythology." In *Kerygma and Myth: A Theological Debate*. Translated by Hans Werner Bartsch, 1-44. New York: Harper & Brothers, 1961.

Caballeros, Harold. "Defeating the Enemy with the Help of Spiritual Mapping." In *Breaking the Strongholds in the City: How to Use Spiritual Mapping to Make Your Prayers More Strategic, Effective, and Targeted*. Ed. C. Peter Wagner, 123-46. Ventura, CA: Regal Books, 1993.

Cullmann, Oscar. "The Subjection of the Invisible Powers." In *Engaging the Enemy*. Ed. C. Peter Wagner, 193-202. Ventura, CA: Regal Books, 1991.

D'Andrade, Roy. "A Prepositional Analysis of U.S. American Beliefs about Illness." In *Meaning in Anthropology*. Ed. Keith Basso and Henry A. Selby, 155-80. Albuquerque, NM: University of New Mexico Press, 1976. Quoted in James P. Spradley. *Ethnographic Interview*. Fort Worth, TX: Harcourt Brace Jovanovich College Pub., 1979, 190.

Daniel, Glyn. "The Personality of Wales." In *Culture and Environment, Essays in Honour of Sir Cyril Fox*. London: Routledge and Kegen Paul, 1963.

Douglas, Mary. "Cultural Bias." In *The Active Voice*. London: Routledge and Kegen Paul, 1982.

Downs, James F., and Hermann K. Leibtreu. "Culture: Man's Ecological Niche." In *Cultural and Social Anthropology: Introductory Reading in Ethnology*. Ed. Peter B. Hammond, 3-20. New York: Macmillan Pub., 1975.

Finger, Thomas N., and Willard M. Swartley. "Deliverance and Bondage: Biblical and Theological Perspectives." In *Essays on Spiritual Bondage and Deliverance*. Occasional Papers No. 11. Ed. Willard M. Swartley, 10-38. Elkhart, IN: Institute of Mennonite Studies, 1988.

Hiebert, Paul G. "The Category Christian in the Mission Task." Chap. in *Anthropological Reflections on Missiological Issues*. Grand Rapids: Baker Book House, 1994.

__. "Epistemological Foundations for Science and Theology." Chap. in *Anthropological Reflections on Missiological Issues*. Grand Rapids: Baker Books, 1994.

__. "Flaw of the Excluded Middle." Chap. in *Anthropological Reflections on Missiological Issues*. Grand Rapids: Baker Books, 1994.

__. "The Gospel in Our Culture: Methods of Social and Cultural Analysis." In *The Church between Gospel and Culture*. Ed. George R. Hunsberger and Craig van Gelder, 139-57. Grand Rapids: Eerdmans Pub., 1996.

__. "Healing and the Kingdom." Chap. in *Anthropological Reflections on Missiological Issues*. Grand Rapids: Baker Books, 1994.

__. "The Missiological Implications of an Epistemological Shift." Chap. in *Anthropological Reflections on Missiological Issues*. Grand Rapids: Baker Books, 1994.

__. "Spiritual Warfare." Chap. in *Anthropological Reflections on Missiological Issues*. Grand Rapids: Baker Books, 1994.

Hoopenworth, Klaus. „Mission in der Auseinandersetzung mit den Mächten in Nichtchristilichen Weltreligionen." In *Mission als Kampf mit den Mächten*. Ed. Klaus W. Müller, 89-102. Bonn: Verlag für Kultur und Wissenschaft, 1994.

Hrangkhuma, F. "How Redemptive Analogies Can Help Churches Grow." *Evangelical Missions Quarterly* 28 (April 1992): 182-87.

Hsu, Francis L. K. "American Core Values and National Character." Chap. in *Psychological Anthropology: Approaches to Culture and Personality*. Homewood, IL: Dorsey, 1961.

The Intercession Working Group Lausanne Committee for World Evangelization. "Statement on Spiritual Warfare." *Urban Mission* (December 1995): 50-53.

Kasier, Walter C., Jr. "Israel's Missionary Call." In *Perspectives on the World Christian Movement: A Reader*. Rev. ed. Ed. Ralph D. Winter and Steven C. Hawthorne, A-25-33. Pasadena, CA: William Carey Library, 1992.

Kluckhohn, Clyde. "Patterning as Exemplified in Navaho Culture. In *Language, Culture and Personality*. Ed. Leslie Spier, 24-36. Wisconsin: Sapier Morrow Fund, 1949.

Kraft, Charles. "Christian Animism or God-given Authority." In *Spiritual Power and Missions: Raising the Issues*. Ed. Edward Rommen, 88-136. Pasadena, CA: William Carey Library, 1995.

Kraft, Charles H. "In Dark Dungeons of Collective Captivity: Response by Charles H. Kraft." In *Wrestling with Dark Angels*. Ed. C. Peter Wagner and F. Douglas Pennoyer, 271-79. Ventura, CA: Regal Books, 1990.

___."What Kind of Encounters Do We Need in Our Christian Witness?" *Evangelical Missions Quarterly* 27 (July 1991): 258-65.

Lawless, Charles, Jr. "Worldview of the Spirit World." *Strategies for Today's Leaders* 29 (Jan. 1997): 7-9.

Lawson, Stephen. "Defeating Territorial Spirits." In *Engaging the Enemy*. Ed. C. Peter Wagner, 29-42. Ventura, CA: Regal Books, 1991.

Mansfield, Stephen. "God's Redemptive Purpose for Nashville." In *Releasing the Destiny: A Spiritual Warfare Manual for Nashville and Country Music*. Nashville: Daniel 1 School of Leadership, 1993.

Müller, Klaus W. "Geschichte der Ethnologie." In *Ethnologie, Einführung und Überblick*. ed. Hans Fischer, 23-56. Berlin: Dietrich Reimer Verlag, 1992.

___. „Power Encounter als Missionsstrategisches Konzept." In *Mission als Kampf mit den Mächten*. Bonn, Germany: Verlag für Kultur und Wissenschaft, 1993, 61-88.

O'Brien, P. T. "Principalities and Powers: Opponents of the Church." In *Biblical Interpretation and the Church, Text and Context*. Ed. D. A. Carson, 110-50. Grand Rapids: Baker Book House, 1984.

Oesterley, W. O. E. "Angelology and Demonology in Early Judaism." In *A Companion to the Bible*. Ed. T. W. Manson, 332-47. Edinburgh: T & T Clark, 1939.

Opler, Morris E. "An Application of the Theory of Themes in Culture." *Journal of the Washington Academy of Science* 36 (1946): 137-65.

___. "Themes as Dynamic Forces in Culture." *American Journal of Sociology* 51 (1945): 198-206.

___. "Component, Assemblage and Themes in Cultural Integration and Differentiation." *American Anthropologist* 61 (1959): 955-64.

Otis, George, Jr. "An Overview of Spiritual Mapping." In *Breaking the Strongholds in the City: How to Use Spiritual Mapping to Make Your Prayers More Strategic, Effective, and Targeted.* Ed. C. Peter Wagner, 29-47. Ventura, CA: Regal Books, 1993.

Pennoyer, F., Douglas. "In Dark Dungeons of Collective Captivity." In *Wrestling with Dark Angels.* Ed. C. Peter Wagner and F. Douglas Pennoyer, 250-70. Ventura, CA: Regal Books, 1990.

Priest, Robert J., Thomas Campbell, and Bradford A. Mullen. "Missiological Syncretism: The New Animistic Paradigm." In *Spiritual Power and Missions: Raising the Issues.* Ed. Edward Rommen, 9-87. Pasadena, CA: William Carey Library, 1995.

Richardson, Don. "Concept Fulfillment." In *Perspectives on the World Christian Movement.* Ed. Ralph D. Winter and Steven C. Hawthorne, C-59-63. Pasadena, CA: William Carey Library, 1981.

Robb, John. "How Satan Works at the Cosmic Level." In *Behind Enemy Lines.* Ed. Charles H. Kraft and Mark White, 165-98. Grand Rapids: Vine Books, 1994.

___. "Satan's Tactics in Building and Maintaining His Kingdom of Darkness." *International Journal of Frontier Missions* 10 (October 1993): 173-84.

Sider, Ron J. "Christ and Power." *International Review of Missions* 69 (January 1980): 8-20.

Sjöberg, Kjell. "Spiritual Mapping for Prophetic Prayer Actions." In *Breaking Strongholds in Your City: How to Use Spiritual Mapping to Make Your Prayers More Strategic, Effective, and Targeted.* Ed. C. Peter Wagner, 97-119. Ventura, CA: Regal Books, 1993.

Stott, John R. W. "Principalities and Powers." In *Spiritual Warfare.* Ed. John Wimber, 147-66. Anaheim, CA: Mercy Pub., 1988.

Tenney, Merrill C., ed. *The Zondervan Pictorial Encyclopedia of the Bible.* Grand Rapids: Regency Reference Library, 1975. S.v. "Nations," by J. Rea.

Thigpen, Paul. "Spiritual Warfare in the Early Church." *Discipleship Journal* 81 (May/June 1994): 29.

van der Toorn, Karel, Bob Becking, and Pieter W. van der Horst, eds. *Dictionary of Deities and Demons in the bible.* New York: E. J. Brill, 1995. S.v. "Demon," by G. J. Riley.

Van Rheenen, Gailyn. "Animism, Secularism, and Theism: Developing a Tripartite Model." *International Journal of Frontier Missions* 10 (October 1993): 169-72.

___. "Cultural Conceptions of Power in Biblical Perspective." *Missiology* 21 (January 1993): 41-53.

Wagner, C. Peter. "Spiritual Warfare." In *Engaging the Enemy*. Ed. C. Peter Wagner, 3-28. Ventura, CA: Regal Books, 1991.

___. "The Visible and the Invisible." In *Engaging the Enemy*. Ed. C. Peter Wagner, 250-79. Ventura, CA: Regal Books, 1991.

Wakley, Mike. "A Critical Look at New 'Key' to Evangelization." *Evangelical Mission Quarterly* 31 (April 1995): 152-65.

Wallace, Anthony F. C. "Revitalization Movements." *American Anthropologist* 48 (March 1956): 264-81.

White, Thomas B. "Understanding Principalities and Powers." In *Engaging the Enemy*. Ed. C. Peter Wagner, 59-68. Ventura, CA: Regal Books, 1991.

Wilford, John Noble. "Revolution in Mapping." *National Geographic* 2 (Feb. 1998): 13.

Yip, Tai M. "Spiritual Mapping: Another Approach." *Evangelical Mission Quarterly* 31 (April 1995): 166-70.

Unpublished Works

Buchmann, Alan. "Cross cultural Evangelism: The Yala People of SE Nigeria." D.Miss. diss., Fuller Theological Seminary, 1990.

Glasser, Arthur F. "Kingdom and Mission." Unpublished manuscript. Fuller Theological Seminary, 1989.

Gordon, Michael. „Territorische Mächte und Geistliche Kampfführung: Eine Biblische Sicht." Unpublished paper, author's file. Predigerseminar Hamburg, 1993.

Hiebert, Paul G., and R. Daniel Shaw. "The Power and the Glory." Unpublished manuscript. Pasadena, CA. Fuller Theological Seminary, School of World Missions, 1993.

Humble, Arnold L. "Power as a Cultural Theme in Java: Its Interaction with Harmony." D.Miss. diss., Fuller Theological Seminary, 1993.

Kraft, Charles H. "Anthropology for Christian Witness." Vol. 2. Unpublished manuscript. Fuller Theological Seminary. Pasadena, CA, 1994.

Kruesi, Martin. "Contemporary Swiss Worldview in the Light of Its Historical Development." M.A.Miss. thesis, Fuller Theological Seminary, 1990.

Nix, David A. "An Examination of the Analysis of Animistic Conversion in *The Kalimantan Kenyah*." Unpublished paper. Southwestern Baptist Theological Seminary, 1994.

Peterson, Brian K. "The Role of Demonic Influence as a Hindrance to Church Growth." Unpublished paper. Southwestern Baptist Theological Seminary, 1994.

Smith, Ebbie C. "Neither Materialists Nor Magicians: Teachings Concerning Spiritual Warfare among Leaders of the Church in History." Unpublished paper. Southwestern Baptist Theological Seminary, 1995.

Van Engen, Charles. "Theological Reflection with Regard to the Resistant." Paper presented to the Evangelical Missiological Society. 20 November 1997, San Francisco.

Wagner, C. Peter. "MC551: Spiritual Issues in Church Growth." Class Syllabus. Pasadena, CA: Fuller School of World Mission, 1994.

White, Tom. "A Model for Discerning, Penetrating, and Overcoming Ruling Principalities and Powers." A paper presented at the Lausanne II in Manila, Spiritual Warfare Track. Photocopy 6. Quoted in Thomas H. McAlpine, Facing the Powers: What Are the Options?, 51. Monrovia, CA: MARC, 1991.

www.ingramcontent.com/pod-product-compliance
Lightning Source LLC
Chambersburg PA
CBHW070948180426
43194CB00041B/1745